HUEY'S
Best Ever
Barbecue
Recipes

HUEY'S
Best Ever
Barbecue
Recipes

IAIN HEWITSON

PHOTOGRAPHY BY GREG ELMS

A SUE HINES BOOK

ALLEN & UNWIN

First published in 2003

A Sue Hines Book
Allen & Unwin Pty Ltd
83 Alexander Street
Crows Nest NSW 2065
Australia
Phone: (61 2) 8425 0100
Fax: (61 2) 9906 2218
Email: frontdesk@allen-unwin.com.au
Web: http://www.allenandunwin.com

National Library of Australia
Cataloguing-in-publication entry:
Hewitson, Iain.
    Huey's best ever barbecue recipes.

    Includes index.
    ISBN 1 74114 175 3.

    1. Barbecue cookery. I. Elms, Greg. II. Title.

    641.5784

Designed by Andrew Cunningham – Studio Pazzo
Food styling by Virginia Dowzer
Typeset by Pauline Haas
Index by Fay Donlevy
Printed in China by Imago
10 9 8 7 6 5 4 3 2 1

The author and publisher wish to thank Adam Brown from
the Agent Group and Shelley Simpson from Mud Australia for
supplying the beautiful Mud products. For worldwide stockists
go to www.mudaustralia.com

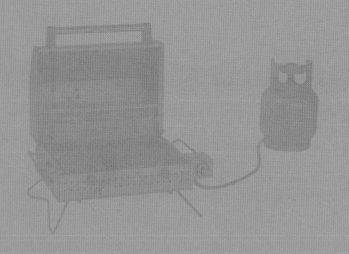

Veal

Red meat

Mince

Sausages

Pork

Cheese

Vegies

The Basics

Thanks

Thanks to Ruth and Charlotte for helping with everything, in particular, the tasting and testing (Charlotte thought the Hot Dogs were cool). Thanks, also to Mosh, Donnelly, Mr Moon, Rob, Noel, Marty, Chris and all the crew at Dreampool, Ruth A. and the team at Tolarno and, once again, to Sue, Andrea, Virginia and Greg for making it all happen.

Top ten BBQ tools

- 🔥 long-handled kitchen tongs (the best are from commercial restaurant suppliers)

- 🔥 cleaning equipment – a stiff brush of course and I also have a large paint scraper which is great for removing obstinate pieces of food

- 🔥 long-handled basting brushes

- 🔥 a selection of spatulas

- 🔥 foil trays, various sizes

- 🔥 a selection of skewers, both metal & wooden

- 🔥 an instant-read meat thermometer

- 🔥 a small folding fan to fan the flames when necessary – an idea from Asia

- 🔥 a water pistol to put out any flare ups (and to discourage pesky guests from interfering at the barbie)

- 🔥 and, of course, lots of tea towels to put in our back pockets for obvious reasons

About barbecuing

In 1492 when Columbus discovered the New World he found the Arawak Indians cooking meat over pits of fire – they called this process *barbacoa* which is, presumably, the origin of what is today known as barbecue.

I will always remember my first attempts at barbecuing. About 10 at the time, I along with my friends Chook Fowler and Spud Taylor, decided that the sausages we had 'borrowed' from Mrs Taylor's pantry would benefit greatly from being cooked over an open fire.

Well, I have to admit that not only were we not terribly good at building a suitable fire (which alternated between foot high flames or none at all) but my brilliant idea of skewering the snags on sharp sticks and holding them over the flames was fine until they were almost cooked, whereby they promptly split and fell into the fire. Still, with a generous application of tomato sauce they tasted pretty damned good; although you would be hard pressed to recognise them as being related to the juicy, succulent little numbers we had started out with.

Since then, thankfully my barbecuing skills have improved somewhat. Burnt offerings are no longer a part of my culinary repertoire and copious quantities of tomato sauce is no longer needed to disguise the disasters. Actually this improvement in backyard cooking skills is not just confined to the Hewitson backyard. Seemingly most Aussies (or at the very least the ones I know) have progressed past their pyromaniac stage and are tossing lots of good things on to their barbies. Whole baby fish, shellfish of all shapes and sizes, tonnes of vegies and every cut of meat imaginable, which is thankfully now trimmed well and cooked without being prodded and turned every second or two.

So welcome to the new world of barbecuing. Sure, this is still the perfect way to entertain a group of friends on a hot, sunny day. But today's barbecue is also an integral part of our kitchen equipment which can be used for everything from family meals to that special dinner party.

And you know what? There is something about the smoky aromas of food being cooked over glowing coals that still, to this day, excites my palate and invariably starts my mouth watering.

How long does it take to cook?

In this book I give very few directions as to how long anything should be cooked. I am not being perverse, it is just that there are so many variables in barbecuing – the BBQ itself, which part of the grill you are cooking on, the thickness of the meat, poultry or seafood, even the weather. So I am going to have to leave it to you, but remember you can cheat a little by making a very small cut in anything with the point of a very small sharp knife and taking a peek (just don't tell anyone I told you this). And, at the risk of repeating myself, for larger joints, whole chickens and the like, an instant-read thermometer is invaluable.

I also have, on the side of my gas-fired BBQ, a burner which certainly makes cooking sauces, blanching vegies and so on a lot easier. But if this is not the case with your barbie, it's worth considering buying one of those small individual units complete with gas bottle which are available in most Asian groceries, camping shops and hardware stores.

The barbecue itself

I have both a kettle and a gas-fired BBQ. Although they are pretty much interchangeable, I tend to use them for particular jobs. For example, I always use the kettle for large pieces of meat, whole chickens and the like, while I prefer to cook steaks, cutlets, fish fillets and all those small numbers on the gas-fired version where the direct heat tends to be fiercer.

And if you don't happen to have a kettle barbecue but instead have a covered oven type gas-fired number, just think of indirect heat as the equivalent of moderate heat, and direct heat as fairly high (in the recipe instructions).

When is it hot enough?

To tell how hot your barbie is, hold your hand about 10 cm above the grill, then start counting until you have to remove your hand – one potato, two potato and so on until four, is a hot fire. Five to six potatoes is medium high, seven to nine is medium, ten to twelve is medium low and thirteen to fifteen is very low and the coals most probably need replenishing.

Starting the feast

Let's be fair, for an everyday meal nothing much apart from good bread is really needed to start proceedings (plus, of course, the best butter or olive oil).

But a quick flash over the coals for that bread plus a vigorous rubbing of a cut garlic clove will make bread even better (as will, in the Spanish style, a similar vigorous rubbing with the fleshy side of a cut tomato). And let us not forget bruschetta, which can be as simple as charred bread topped with diced tomato, onion and basil with a splash of good oil, or as complicated as a ragout of exotic mushrooms or braised artichokes on top.

There will be be occasions when you need to pull out all the stops and wow the mob. In this instance I often just buy a selection of fresh seafood – prawns in the shell, freshly shucked oysters, crabs, yabbies, bugs etc – and serve the lot on ice with plenty of napkins, finger bowls and a selection of sauces.

An antipasto platter is always a hit too. I have to admit I cheat a little, dash into my favourite deli and pile my platter with goodies such as pâtés, terrines, sliced prosciutto and salami, Persian feta, various dips, marinated olives and whatever else takes my fancy. I then add some homemade stuff such as asparagus wrapped in prosciutto (or smoked salmon) with horseradish sour cream (see page 94), barbecued vegies in the Spanish style (see page 90), roasted capsicums (see page 110) or, in fact, almost any of the vegetable dishes that start on page 90. I even, when I'm feeling generous, throw on some of the aforementioned fresh seafood, once again breaking out the napkins, fingerbowls and sauces.

And may I suggest, after all this amazing effort, if the guests aren't suitably impressed I recommend that you:

(a) Never invite them again.
(b) Eat the lot yourself.

Squid or calamari

... in a Vietnamese salad

4–8 squid or calamari tubes, cleaned
vegetable oil spray

Cut each tube into 4–6 even pieces. Score in a diamond pattern and blanch in boiling water for 30 seconds. Drain well, spray generously with oil and BBQ over a very high heat until lightly charred.

---

1 garlic clove, crushed
1 tbsp Asian fish sauce
juice of 1–2 limes
a splash of Chinese rice wine
1 heaped tspn shaved palm sugar
a splash of sesame oil
2 chillies, finely sliced

Whisk.

3–4 baby carrots, peeled & sliced
½ red capsicum, cored, seeded & finely sliced
½ cup coriander leaves
½ cup mint leaves
4 tbsp peanuts roasted (see below)

Blanch vegetables for 30 seconds in boiling water and put in a separate bowl. Add herbs, peanuts and squid and toss with dressing to taste.

To pan-roast peanuts

toss raw peanuts in a dry pan on the barbie until slightly charred, rolling as you do so.

Squid or calamari

... with spicy salt, chilli & garlic on charred baby bok choy

¼ cup vegetable oil 2 garlic cloves, crushed 1 tbsp soy sauce 1 tbsp Chinese rice wine a pinch of sugar	Combine.
6 squid or calamari tubes, cleaned	Cut each tube into 4–6 even pieces. Score in a diamond pattern and blanch in boiling water for 30 seconds. Drain well, then add to marinade, toss and leave for 30 minutes.
1 garlic clove, finely chopped 2 chillies, seeded & finely chopped 1 tbsp spicy salt (see below) 1 tbsp Chinese rice wine ½ tbsp grated fresh ginger 3 spring (green) onions, finely diced	In a medium pan on the BBQ, heat a little of marinade and sauté briefly. Set aside.
4–8 baby bok choy, cleaned & halved lengthways oil spray	Spray and cook on BBQ until lightly charred. When almost ready, toss squid on and cook briefly, brushing with marinade. Then put squid into pan, return to heat and toss for a minute or two. Put bok choy on a platter, top with squid and sprinkle contents of pan over the top.

To make spicy salt

combine 1 tbsp Szechwan peppercorns and 3 tbsp sea salt in a small pan and put over heat until the mix begins to crackle. Remove, cool and grind in a mortar or a spice mill.

Crustaceans

. . . crayfish (lobster) with a roasted capsicum butter

Certainly not for the diet conscious.

2 red capsicums, roasted & peeled (see page 110)
2 anchovies
150 gm soft unsalted butter
½ tbsp chopped parsley
freshly ground salt & pepper

Whiz up capsicums and anchovies in a processor. Add to butter in a bowl with parsley and seasonings and, with your hands, mix gently.

2–4 green crayfish tails

Cut in half lengthways and remove track. Then cook flesh side down on hot BBQ for 3 minutes. Turn over and smear generously with the butter, move to moderate part of the BBQ and cook, covered, adding more butter as you do so. When ready (to check, make a small cut in flesh) remove.

1–2 bunches watercress, washed

Scatter over plates or a platter. Put crays on top and add a few more dollops of the butter on top.

My mate Bob Hart

wrote in a recent column about his favourite way to prepare mudcrabs. Simply wash well, wrap in double foil with a chunk of butter and a glug of white wine and cook in a kettle or covered BBQ – sounds wonderful to me.

Crustaceans

... prawns stuffed with a South-East Asian herb pesto

2 tbsp vegetable oil
2 garlic cloves, crushed
4 chillies, seeded & chopped
1 cm piece fresh ginger, grated
1 tbsp grated lemongrass
3 heaped tbsp chopped coriander
a good splash Asian fish sauce
1 tspn shaved palm sugar

Whiz up in a processor until a paste forms.

---

1 kilo green, jumbo king prawns

With a sharp knife or small scissors, cut along back of shell also cutting out a little bit of flesh. Remove vein with point of knife and spoon a little of mix under shell. Refrigerate for at least one hour. Then barbecue over a high heat until prawns turn a pinky-red colour.

Skewer the prawns individually lengthways

if you like – it certainly makes the cooking process 'simpler'.

Molluscs

... oysters with a splash of Thai vinaigrette

½ cup coriander leaves
6 coriander roots, washed well
4 garlic cloves
4 chillies, chopped
1 tbsp Asian fish sauce
1 tbsp shaved palm sugar
1 tspn rock salt
juice of 3 limes

Blend.

2–3 dozen oysters in the shell, scrubbed

Put on the hottest part of the BBQ and cook until they open. Then add a splash of vinaigrette to each. (Or instead, you could just add a squeeze of fresh lime juice.)

Keep a small knife handy

(or an oyster knife) because the oysters may need a little help. If the juices begin to bubble around the edges before they open, slip the knife in and give the shell a twist.

Molluscs

. . . scallops on the half shell with lemon & chilli oil

1 cup olive oil
4 red chillies, seeded & finely chopped
zest of 1 lemon
juice of 2 lemons
2 garlic cloves, crushed
freshly ground salt & pepper

Heat oil in a small pot, add rest of ingredients, turn off heat and leave for 3–4 hours.

12–16 fresh scallops in the half shell, firmly attached

Preheat grill plate. Sprinkle the oil mix generously over the scallops and then cook, upside down, for 30 seconds (if not firmly attached or if they are very small just cook flesh up). Turn over, sprinkle with more oil and cook for another 30 seconds. Sprinkle with more oil and serve.

. . . a parcel of mussels 'mariniere'

Pre-prepare these parcels and just throw them on the barbie when your guests are in need of sustenance.

40–50 fresh mussels, scrubbed & de-bearded (see page 110)
1 medium onion, finely chopped
2 heaped tbsp chopped parsley
2 garlic cloves, crushed
dry white wine

Preheat kettle BBQ with direct heat (see page 50). Put mussels on 4 large squares of doubled foil. Scatter onion, parsley and garlic over the top and then add a good splash of white wine to each. Fold up and crimp foil and cook, covered, for about 10 minutes until mussels open. Serve in bowls with juices poured over top. Discard any unopened mussels.

To clean scallops

carefully remove black track with a small sharp knife then gently wash and dry.

Tuna steaks

. . . with Provençale vegies & a red capsicum aioli

2 each yellow & red capsicums, seeded
  & cored
3 zucchini
1 medium eggplant
olive oil
freshly ground salt & pepper

Cut vegetables into neat even pieces. Toss with oil and seasonings and barbecue until tender and lightly charred.

---

olive oil
freshly ground salt & pepper
4 x 180 gm tuna steaks, trimmed of bloodline
red capsicum aioli (see page 114)

When vegetables are almost ready, oil, season and barbecue over a high heat to no more than medium-rare. Then scatter vegies on plates or a platter, top with tuna and add a dollop of aioli on each.

. . . peppered with a Middle Eastern vegetable stew

Mixed pepper is available in small grinders in the spice section of supermarkets.

4 x 180 gm thick tuna steaks, trimmed
  of bloodline
mixed pepper

Generously coat both sides with freshly ground mixed pepper and set aside.

---

olive oil
1–2 red onions, cut in wedges
2 garlic cloves, crushed
1 each red & green capsicum, cored,
  seeded & sliced
2 Japanese eggplant, sliced
2 cans chopped tomatoes
½ cup chicken stock (bought is fine)
1 can chickpeas, drained & rinsed
freshly ground salt & pepper

Heat oil in a medium, heavy-based pot and sauté onions and garlic until soft. Then add capsicums and eggplant and sauté for a few more minutes. Add tomatoes, stock and seasoning and cook gently until thick and fragrant. Add chickpeas and keep warm on the side of the BBQ.

---

olive oil spray
harissa yoghurt (see page 112)

When ready to serve, spray tuna, and barbecue over a high heat to medium-rare. Serve on a mound of vegetable stew with a sprinkling of yoghurt.

Tuna steaks

... with chorizo, potatoes & a semi-dried tomato dressing

1 tbsp Dijon mustard
1 garlic clove, crushed
150 ml olive oil
6 semi-dried tomatoes (& a little bit
   of their oil)
1 anchovy
freshly ground pepper

Whiz up in a food processor or blender.

2–3 chorizo sausages, sliced on the diagonal
8 baby potatoes, scrubbed, halved & boiled
   until almost tender

Cook on an oiled BBQ grill plate until crusty.

---

4 x 180 gm thick tuna steaks, bloodline
   removed
olive oil spray
sea salt

Spray with oil, season and barbecue over a high
heat to medium-rare.

---

chopped parsley

Put potatoes and chorizo on plates or a platter, top
with tuna and sprinkle with dressing and parsley.

Treat tuna like the steak of the sea

and don't overcook – otherwise it will be dry and tasteless. Also buy sashimi-grade

tuna if possible. It's certainly more expensive, but the flavour is so much better.

Swordfish or marlin steaks

. . . on BBQ spring onions with a putanesca salsa

The most important thing about making a good salsa is to ensure that
the ingredients are evenly and neatly chopped or diced.

6 tbsp olive oil ½ red onion, chopped 2 garlic cloves, crushed 2 chillies, seeded & finely sliced	In a small pan on the BBQ, heat oil and gently sauté vegetables. Put in a bowl.
4 anchovies, chopped 6 tomatoes, peeled, seeded & diced (see page 110) 6 pitted black olives, sliced 12 capers, rinsed 8 basil leaves, sliced 4 tbsp freshly grated parmesan	Add to bowl, toss well and set aside.
4 x 180 gm swordfish or marlin steaks olive oil spray freshly ground salt & pepper	Oil and season fish. Then barbecue over a high heat.
olive oil spray 1–2 bunches large spring (green) onions, cleaned	At the same time, spray onions and toss on BBQ, cooking until slightly charred all over. Put on plates or a platter and top with fish and salsa.

Just for your culinary edification

salsas (Mexican and Latin American), sambals (Asian) and salsitas (Cuban) are pretty

much the same beast – a mixture of diced vegies and/or fruit along with gutsy

flavours such as chillies, garlic and ginger and a splash of something to moisten the

lot. But just to confuse the issue, in Asia there is sambal oelek which is a puree of

chillies and in Italy we find salsa verde which is more pesto in style.

Swordfish or marlin steaks

... with a pineapple sambal

The easiest way to prepare fresh pineapple is using pastry cutters. Just cut the pineapple in slices, skin and all. Then, using a large cutter, press it firmly through the flesh just inside the skin, then using a small cutter, remove core.

8 slices fresh pineapple, cored & diced 2 chillies, seeded & sliced 1 garlic clove, finely chopped 1 heaped tspn grated fresh ginger juice of 1–2 limes freshly ground salt & pepper	Toss together in a bowl and set aside for 15 minutes.
4 x 180 gm swordfish or marlin steaks vegetable oil spray	Spray fish with oil, season and barbecue over a high heat.
lime wedges	Serve with a spoon of sambal and lime wedges.

... with a Cuban pawpaw salsita

¼ cup olive oil ½ small red onion, chopped 2 chillies, seeded & sliced	Cook in a small pan over a low heat for a few minutes.
½ medium pawpaw, peeled, seeded & diced zest & juice of 1–2 limes zest & juice of 1 orange 6–8 mint leaves, sliced	Put in a bowl, pour hot oil mix over and leave for 30 minutes to develop flavours.
4 x 180 gm swordfish or marlin steaks olive oil spray freshly ground salt & pepper	Spray with oil, season and barbecue over high heat. Scatter salsita over plates and top with fish steaks.

Salmon steaks or fillets

... in a BLT sandwich

½ cup mayonnaise 3 tbsp sour cream 3 tbsp chopped fresh basil zest & juice of ½ lemon	Mix.
4 x 100 gm salmon steaks, boned & skinned 1 lemon olive oil spray sea salt	Season and spray with oil. Then barbecue, squeezing over lemon juice as you do so.
4 rindless bacon rashers 8 thick slices of sourdough bread	At the same time, cook bacon and, when fish is almost ready, the bread. Lay 4 slices of bread on the bench and smear generously with mayo.
3 ripe, red tomatoes, thickly sliced 1 red onion, finely sliced inner leaves of a cos lettuce	Top with tomato, onion, lettuce, salmon, bacon and more mayo and then the other slices of bread.

Ask your fishmonger to remove the pin bones

or at least show you where they are, so you can remove them with tweezers or a small pair of pliers.

Salmon steaks or fillets

... paillards with whipped lime & coriander butter

100 gm soft unsalted butter zest of 1 lime juice of 2 limes 3 tbsp chopped coriander	Whisk in a bowl and set aside.
8 x 100 gm slices of fresh salmon, boned & skinned	Top with doubled-over kitchen wrap and gently batten out.
olive oil spray freshly ground salt & pepper	When ready to serve, spray with oil, season and cook very briefly on hot grill plate. Top with a dollop of butter and serve.

... in a warm Provençale salad with anchovy mayo

8 baby potatoes, well scrubbed table salt 12–16 baby green beans, topped, tailed & halved crossways	Cook spuds in salted water. When ready, add beans for a minute. Drain and cut potatoes in half.
2 x 200 gm salmon steaks, boned & skinned	When potatoes are almost ready, barbecue salmon on a hot oiled grill until crusty on the outside but still opaque in centre. Then flake into a bowl with potatoes and beans.
4 eggs, soft boiled & halved 12–16 pitted black olives 12 cherry tomatoes, halved a good handful baby rocket olive oil anchovy mayo (see page 114)	Add along with a little oil. Toss gently, mound in a bowl and sprinkle with mayo. Serve rest of mayo on the side.

Preparing for the great moment

🔥 Make sure the grate and grill plate are clean. To do this, bring it up to heat, scrub thoroughly (in the case of the grate, with a stiff wire brush) and rub with a well-oiled cloth. Then wait until any flames die down before barbecuing.

🔥 Remove barbecue items from the fridge at least 30 minutes before cooking to bring them to room temperature. They will then cook more quickly and evenly.

🔥 Check that you have the barbecue paraphernalia nearby, that is, tongs, gloves, spatula, BEER, sauces, bastes, knives and the like. Because if you suddenly discover that you have forgotten any such essentials, your barbie could quickly turn into a disaster as you dash inside, attempting to rectify the situation.

🔥 And while on the subject of essentials, a bucket of sand or coarse salt or even a garden hose should be nearby in case of mishaps (a fire blanket is also a good choice).

🔥 Also another important point: the barbecue is not a place for small children or pets, so please keep them clear. And while shorts and skimpy clothing are part of the barbie tradition, a large apron and covered shoes are not a bad idea in case of burning embers.

These days

most Aussies (or at the very
least the ones I know) have
progressed past their
pyromaniac stage.

Salmon steaks or fillets

... tea-smoked with sauce vierge

**4 ripe red tomatoes, peeled, seeded & diced
(see page 110)
1 cup olive oil
juice of 1–2 lemons
8–10 basil leaves, sliced
rock salt**

Mix together and set aside.

**30 gm Lapsang Souchong tea leaves
30 gm normal tea leaves
120 gm short grain rice
100 gm brown sugar
2 rosemary stalks**

Preheat kettle BBQ and then scatter coals evenly over grid (see page 50). Mix teas, rice, sugar and rosemary together and put in a large foil pan on top of coals. Heat until this begins to smoulder.

**6–8 x 180 gm salmon steaks,
boned & skinned**

Oil rack well and place salmon on top. Cover and close vents to ¼. Cook until salmon is opaque in centre (check with a small knife) then put on a platter or plates and top with a generous amount of sauce.

This works brilliantly with a whole salmon

or ocean trout – and try using different varieties of tea.

White fish fillets

... wrapped in banana leaves with a green coconut chutney

2 cups dessicated coconut 1 cup coconut cream 2 tspn turmeric 1 tspn cumin seeds 2 tbsp Indian mango chutney 2 chillies, chopped 2 tbsp grated lemongrass 2 garlic cloves, crushed 1 cm piece fresh ginger, grated juice of 1 lime 1 cup mint leaves 1 cup coriander leaves	Whiz up in a processor.
2 banana leaves	Cut into 8 even, largish pieces and dip in boiling water for a few seconds to soften. Then drain.
8 x 120 gm fish fillets freshly ground salt juice of 1 fresh lime kitchen string	Place banana leaves on the bench, top with fish and season with salt and lime juice. Spread chutney evenly on top, fold up banana leaves (seams underneath) and tie with kitchen string (this can be done beforehand). When ready to serve, put on BBQ, cover with lid or foil tray and cook until firm when pressed.
raita (see page 112)	Unwrap and sprinkle with raita.

A common mistake is to overcrowd the barbie

Not only does it make it difficult to turn anything, but also to move any item that is cooking too quickly or too slowly. It is also important, for even cooking, that the heat rises around the edges of the food.

White fish fillets

... Sicilian-stuffed shashliks on a tangy tomato salad

600 gm large steaky fish fillets, such as blue-eye or groper	Cut into 12 even slices and gently batten out under doubled-over kitchen wrap. Trim until reasonably square and finely chop any scraps.
olive oil **½ onion, chopped** **2 garlic cloves, crushed**	Heat a little oil in a medium pan and sauté along with fish scraps until tender. Put in a bowl.
8 wooden skewers, pre-soaked in cold water for 30 minutes **1 cup dried breadcrumbs** **½ cup grated parmesan** **1 egg** **2 tbsp chopped basil** **1 tspn capers, drained** **3 anchovies, chopped** **grated zest of 1 lemon** **2 tbsp chopped black olives**	Add to onion mix and mix well. Spoon some onto centre of each piece of fish and roll up (don't overstuff). Place 3 rolls alongside each other on board and put 2 wooden skewers through them crossways. Repeat process and barbecue over a moderately high heat on a well-oiled grill.
6–8 ripe red tomatoes, cored & sliced **extra virgin olive oil** **balsamic vinegar** **sea salt** **lemon wedges**	Put tomatoes on plates or a platter. Sprinkle with oil, vinegar and salt. Top with shashliks and serve with lemon wedges.

This method of double-skewering

ensures that these fish rolls will not come apart when turning – and, apart from that,

it makes them a lot easier to flip over.

White fish steaks or cutlets

... with a Mediterranean slaw & caperberry butter

If you can't find caperberries, plain old-fashioned capers will do.

1 radicchio, well washed & sliced	Toss with oil, balsamic and seasoning, to taste.
1 witloof, well washed & sliced	
2 tbsp walnut halves	
olive oil	
balsamic vinegar	
freshly ground salt & pepper	

4 x 180 gm fish fillets	Season fish and cook on an oiled BBQ, squeezing lemon juice over as you do so.
1 lemon	

100 gm unsalted butter	While fish is cooking, put in a pan or small pot and melt over the hot part of BBQ. Scatter salad on a platter or plates, top with fish and pour butter over the top.
2 tbsp caperberries	
1 tbsp chopped parsley	
a squeeze of lemon juice	

I tend to use more robust varieties of fish

such as blue-eye, groper, snapper and the like when barbecuing. But if a more delicate variety such as whiting is the best available, leave the skin on and cook it briefly, skin-side down first on a well-oiled grill plate.

Whole baby fish

. . . in foil with lemon & fennel

**4 plate-sized whole baby fish, cleaned
& scaled**
olive oil spray
freshly ground salt & pepper
2–3 large lemons, 1 sliced
fennel leaves (or dill)

Cut 3 diagonal slashes in each fish. Cut lemon slices in half and put in slashes. Then squeeze juice over the top and season. Oil 4 squares of foil, top with fish and scatter with fennel. Then wrap up tightly, leaving a space above fish and cook on BBQ. (To check if cooked, unwrap and make a small cut behind heads.)

. . . with soy, ginger & spring onion

**4 plate-sized whole baby fish, cleaned
& scaled**
4 cm piece ginger, peeled & finely sliced
4 spring (green) onions, finely sliced
Japanese soy sauce

Oil 4 squares of foil, top with fish, scatter with ginger and spring onions and sprinkle generously with soy. Then wrap up tightly, leaving a space above fish, and cook on BBQ. (To check if cooked, unwrap and make a small cut behind heads.)

Serve fish with corn in the husk

with lime & coriander butter (see page 96) – delicious.

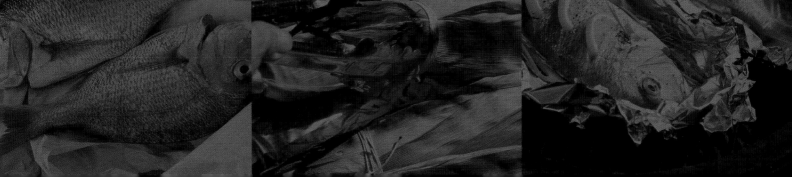

Whole baby fish

... Szechwan style

**4 plate-sized whole baby fish, cleaned
  & scaled**
Chinese rice wine
Japanese soy sauce
**4 heads bok choy, cleaned & halved
  lengthways**

Cut 3 diagonal slashes in each fish, put on oiled squares of foil and sprinkle generously with rice wine and soy. Top with bok choy, wrap up tightly, leaving a space above fish, and cook on BBQ.

6 tbsp peanut oil
6 tspn sesame oil
2 garlic cloves, crushed
1 tspn grated fresh ginger
2 heaped tspn Asian chilli bean sauce
4 spring (green) onions, finely chopped

When fish is ready, heat oils in a medium pan on BBQ until smoking. Then add rest of ingredients together with fish juices and mix.

Place fish on plates, top with bok choy and pour oil over the lot.

Sydney chef Tony Bilson has an interesting recipe in his book *Fine Family Cooking,* which involves wrapping a whole fish in wet newspaper (after stuffing it with lemon slices, herbs, butter & quartered onions) and then burying it in the hot coals and covering it with more hot coals. I gave the recipe a shot and ended up, after peeling off any newspaper which hadn't burnt off by itself, with the most delicious, moist, flavoursome fish.

Whole baby fish

... Spanish-style sardines with aioli & a chickpea & carrot salad

4–6 baby carrots, peeled & sliced on the
   diagonal
1–2 cans chickpeas, drained & rinsed well
1–2 tspn smoked paprika
1 tspn ground cinnamon
1 tspn cumin
zest of 1 lemon
juice of 2 lemons
1 chilli, seeded & finely sliced
2 tbsp honey
⅓–½ cup olive oil

Cook carrots in salted boiling water for a few
minutes. Then drain, toss with the rest and set aside.

---

24 whole sardines, cleaned & gutted
sea salt
olive oil spray

Sprinkle generously with salt, pressing firmly into
skin. Then spray with oil and cook briefly on a hot
grill plate.

---

aioli (see page 114)

Scatter salad on plates or a platter, top with sardines
and dollops of aioli.

Dipping a branch of rosemary in oil
and brushing the food with it as it cooks, adds a wonderful extra bit of flavour.

Chicken bits

... in a spicy citrus marinade with banana & mango chutney

½ cup soft herb leaves, such as coriander, mint & parley 1 tbsp Dijon mustard 2 garlic cloves, crushed 4 chillies, chopped juice of 1 lime juice of 2 oranges a splash of soy sauce	Whiz up in a blender or processor. Put in a bowl.
chilli vinegar, bought freshly ground pepper 12–18 boneless chicken thighs	Add vinegar and pepper to taste. Then throw in chicken and refrigerate overnight.
olive oil 4 spring (green) onions, finely sliced 1 chilli, seeded & sliced	Heat a little oil in a pot and briefly toss.
1 tspn hot Indian curry paste a good pinch turmeric	Add and toss for a minute or two.
3 very ripe bananas, roughly mashed 200 ml canned mango, chopped juice of 1½ oranges juice of 1 lime 1 tspn sugar	Add and cook gently until thick and fragrant.
10 mint leaves, sliced chilli vinegar, bought	Turn off, add mint and vinegar to taste. Set aside.
	When ready to serve, cook chicken, covered in a kettle BBQ over direct heat (see page 50), brushing with marinade regularly (or on a normal BBQ with a foil pan over the top). Serve with a good dollop of chutney.

Chicken bits

... drumsticks, Thai style

SERVES
4

1 bunch coriander, including roots,
   washed well & roughly chopped
5 garlic cloves, crushed
5 chillies, chopped
2 tspn shaved palm sugar
2 tspn rock salt
freshly ground pepper
juice of 3 limes

Whiz up in a processor (adding a little vegie oil if necessary). Put in a large bowl.

12 drumsticks

Toss in marinade and refrigerate overnight, turning 2 or 3 times. Then barbecue, covered, in a kettle BBQ over direct heat, brushing with marinade regularly.

... a pile of wings

SERVES
6–8

To ensure that you don't get cross-contamination with chicken, it is best to stop brushing with marinade 10 or so minutes before it is ready.

1½ cups vegetable oil
1 tbsp honey
1 tbsp mustard
2 tspn sambal oelek
2 garlic cloves, crushed
1 cm piece fresh ginger, grated
juice of 2 lemons
½ cup kecap manis

Whisk in a bowl.

30–40 chicken wings

Prepare by cutting off tips (and discarding) and then cutting in half at joint. Toss in marinade and refrigerate overnight, mixing a few times.

Next day, cook on an oiled BBQ plate, brushing generously with marinade as you do so.

Chicken bits

... jerked chicken with candied sweet potatoes

6 spring (green) onions, finely chopped 3 chillies, finely chopped 4 garlic cloves, finely chopped ¼ cup vegetable oil ¼ cup fresh lime juice 2 tbsp soy sauce 2 tspn allspice 2 tspn fresh thyme leaves	Whisk.
4 chicken marylands (or 8 thighs)	Toss in a bowl, mix well and marinate for at least 1 hour.
2–3 sweet potatoes, scrubbed well	Boil until just tender when pierced with a skewer. Cool and then cut into thick slices.
honey	Preheat kettle BBQ (see page 50). Cook chicken, covered, over direct heat, brushing with marinade and turning regularly. Melt honey in a small pot or pan and, when chicken is almost ready, cook sweet potatoes, brushing with honey for the last few minutes.

The process of jerking meat and poultry
was originally brought to the West Indies by the Arawak Indians from South America. And, whilst there are many 'authentic' versions, the one thing that the locals do agree on is that the marinade must be heavily laced with chillies and allspice and the meat should be semi-smoked in a kettle BBQ.

Chicken breasts

... Asian-marinated with snowpea & spring onion salad

½ cup soy sauce
½ cup mirin (Japanese rice wine)
6 tbsp Chinese rice wine
3 tbsp vegetable oil
2 tspn sugar
3 spring (green) onions, finely sliced

Whisk and keep one quarter aside.

6–8 skinless boned chicken breast fillets

Toss in three quarters of mix and mix well. Leave for 2–3 hours, turning a few times. Then barbecue on an oiled grill, brushing with marinade as you do so.

30–40 baby snowpeas, topped & tailed
4–6 spring (green) onions, cleaned & cut into 2 cm lengths

When chicken is ready, either blanch very briefly in boiling water or toss in a hot oiled wok.

Scatter vegetables on a platter. Cut each breast into 3 crossways, pile on top and sprinkle with the reserved marinade.

Chicken breasts

... Thai cakes with a sweet chilli sauce

½ red capsicum, cored, seeded & chopped 2 cm piece fresh ginger, grated 2 garlic cloves, crushed 3 tbsp Asian hot chilli sauce	Whiz up in a processor.
500 gm skinless chicken breast, cubed 75 ml coconut cream	Add and process until smooth.
1 egg freshly ground salt & pepper	Add and whiz for a few seconds. Remove to a bowl.
6 spring (green) onions, chopped ½ bunch coriander, chopped	Mix in and refrigerate for an hour or more.
flour vegetable oil	Form into patties (about 4 cm x 1 cm thick) and flour lightly. (Do this carefully because at this stage the mix will be a bit soft.) Oil grill plate and cook until golden.
1 continental (telegraph) cucumber, sliced 　on the diagonal Asian sweet chilli sauce Thai slaw (see page 98)	Put cucumber on plates or a platter, top with cakes, sprinkle with sauce and serve with slaw on the side.

Always preheat the BBQ

whether gas- or coal-fired. And to give you some flexibility in your cooking, keep one part cooler than the other and move any food that is browning too quickly to that more moderate section. Also, if your BBQ doesn't have a cover, keep large foil trays or a wok cover handy to plop over the top and create an oven-like effect.

Chicken breasts

. . . a lime-flavoured paillard with tomato & coriander salsa

4 boneless, skinless chicken breasts	Batten out to an even thickness under doubled over kitchen wrap. Neaten with a sharp knife.
½ cup olive oil **zest of 1 lime** **juice of 3 limes** **freshly ground salt & pepper**	Whisk, pour over chicken and leave for 30 minutes, turning once or twice.
2 punnets cherry tomatoes, halved **1 small red onion, finely sliced** **3 tbsp chopped coriander** **2 tbsp olive oil** **juice of 2 limes** **a good splash of green Tabasco**	Mix together and set aside to develop flavours.
	Barbecue chicken, brushing with marinade as you do so. Serve with a good dollop of salsa on top.

A paillard

is any cut of meat, poultry or fish which is cut thinly and is of an even thickness,

enabling it to be cooked quickly and easily.

Whole chickens

... cooked on a beer can

2 handfuls of woodchips
1 large chicken
1 can beer

Soak woodchips overnight. Set kettle BBQ to indirect grilling with large drip tray in centre (see page 50). Open beer and pour off (or drink) half. Insert can in the chicken's cavity and spread legs so that it will be steady on the grill.

spice mix (try McCormick's spicy Italian)
olive oil spray

Sprinkle generously with spice mix and place chicken upright over drip tray. Put a handful of drained chips on each bed of coals, cover and cook for about $3/4$ hour, spraying every now and then with oil.

2 handfuls baby rocket
olive oil
balsamic

When ready (check by piercing thigh with table fork – when juices should run clear) remove can carefully, joint and serve with a pile of oil and vinegar dressed leaves.

This American classic sounds weird

but if you try no other recipe in this book, give this one a shot because it produces a wonderful moist, juicy, flavoursome bird with a terrific crispy skin. And while we're on the subject, American BBQ guru, Steven Raichlen, suggests another even weirder number. For a low-brow version of duck a l'orange, simply put a can of Fanta inside a duck and proceed as above.

Whole chickens

. . . finger licking spatchcocks

4 baby chickens
8 wooden skewers, soaked in cold water for
  30 minutes (or metal skewers)

With kitchen scissors, cut along each side of the backbone. Turn over, place on board and give a good whack with the palm of your hand to flatten. Then thread each with 2 skewers in the form of a cross.

---

1 cup olive oil
zest of 1 lemon
juice of 2 lemons
1 heaped tspn honey
1 tspn sambal oelek
1 heaped tspn Dijon mustard
a good splash of soy sauce

Whisk, pour over chickens and marinate overnight, turning 3 or 4 times.

Preheat kettle BBQ with direct heat (see page 50). Place spatchcocks on hottest part, cover, and cook, brushing with marinade and turning regularly until well-coloured. Then move to a more moderate part of the grill. And, to speed up the cooking process, flatten the birds even more by wrapping bricks in foil and whacking them on top. (To check if the birds are ready, pierce the thighs with a fork – when the juices run clear they are done.)

You can also cook these on a normal BBQ

but they will need to be covered with either a wok lid or large foil trays to ensure they cook right through.

Quail

... Moroccan pot-barbecued with preserved lemons & raisins

This appears to be a rather strange BBQ recipe but the end result will surprise and will be a wonderful contrast to the tons of grilled food that is taking up most of the table. And if you can't find (or can't be bothered to make) preserved lemons, just use sliced fresh lemon.

---

8 whole jumbo quails
freshly ground salt & pepper
olive oil spray

Set kettle BBQ for slowish indirect cooking (see page 50). Tuck quail wings under bodies, push toothpicks through legs and points of breast, season and spray with oil, then barbecue briefly until coloured on all sides.

---

2 cups chicken stock (bought is fine)
2 tbsp raisins
4 pieces preserved lemon, flesh removed & discarded, skin finely sliced
2 garlic cloves, crushed
1 tspn turmeric
freshly ground salt & pepper
1 tbsp harissa, bought or homemade (see page 111)

Put in a large heavy-bottomed pot large enough to hold quails in one layer (and also able to fit under cover of BBQ). Add quails, breast side up, put on BBQ, cover and cook very gently for about 20 minutes, turning 2 or 3 times.

---

1 cup orange juice
1 tspn ground cinnamon
2 tbsp olive oil
1 small zucchini, diced
4 baby carrots, sliced

Bring to the boil in a saucepan. (Make the couscous while the quails are cooking, or prepare it beforehand and reheat in microwave when needed.) Remove from heat.

---

1 cup couscous
2 tbsp raisins

Pour over the top of the hot orange juice mix and stir through. Leave for 5 minutes.

---

a dollop of soft butter

Stir butter into couscous and fluff with a fork.

---

2 tbsp chopped coriander

Remove quails from pot when ready, take out toothpicks and place on a bed of couscous. Over a high heat, reduce sauce a little, add coriander and pour over the top.

Quail

... butterflied with Algerian flavours

8 whole jumbo quails

Using kitchen scissors, cut along each side of backbone. Then, with fingers, remove ribs and backbone and flatten with palm of your hand.

1 cup olive oil
zest & juice of 1 lemon
2 garlic cloves, crushed
1 cm piece fresh ginger, grated
2 chillies, seeded & sliced
1 tspn pomegranate molasses
1 tspn sumac
1 tspn paprika
1 heaped tspn fresh thyme leaves

Whisk, pour over quails and marinate for at least 2–3 hours.

lime wedges

Barbecue over a high heat, brushing with marinade, until crusty and golden. Serve with lime wedges.

Sumac & pomegranate molasses

are available in Middle Eastern delis and food stores.

Lamb cutlets

... Moroccan chermoula marinated with Turkish eggplant salad

4 garlic cloves, crushed 2 cm piece fresh ginger, grated 1 tspn saffron threads, soaked in a little hot water ½ cup fresh coriander leaves ½ cup fresh mint leaves 1 cup olive oil 1 tbsp honey 1 tbsp sambal oelek freshly ground salt & pepper juice of 2–3 lemons	Blend.
18–24 lamb cutlets, French trimmed	Toss in marinade and leave for at least an hour or two. Then barbecue, brushing with marinade as you do so.
1 cup plain yoghurt 1 heaped tbsp harissa, bought or homemade (see page 111) a squeeze of lemon juice Turkish eggplant salad (see page 99)	Mix yoghurt, harissa and lemon together. Put cutlets on a bed of salad, sprinkle with yoghurt mixture and serve with eggplant salad.

A typical Huey mishmash of cultures
but it tastes good and isn't that all that matters?

Lamb cutlets

... 'scottadito' with charred bread & tomato salad

12–18 lamb cutlets, French trimmed
½ cup olive oil
juice of 1 lemon
freshly ground salt & pepper

Put cutlets on a plate and pour over oil and lemon juice. Season and turn to coat well.

8–12 thick slices country-style bread
6 large ripe, red tomatoes cored & thickly sliced
olive oil spray

Spray bread and tomatoes. Then barbecue until slightly charred. Remove and cube.

1–2 chillies, seeded & finely sliced
1 small red onion, finely sliced
12 basil leaves, torn in 2 or 3
balsamic vinegar
olive oil
freshly ground salt & pepper

Toss chillies, onion and basil with above, adding balsamic, oil and seasoning to taste.

---

lemon wedges

Cook cutlets, brushing with marinade as you do so. Serve with a mound of salad and lemon wedges.

A traditional Italian favourite

Scottadito means burning fingers which is exactly what happens when you attempt to eat them with your little pinkies (as is also traditional).

Loin of lamb

. . . skewered with onion, a feta cheese salad & sauce tzatziki

½ cup olive oil
juice of ½–1 lemon
½ cup fresh herb leaves (parsley, mint
   & basil)
1 garlic clove, crushed
freshly ground salt & pepper

Whiz up in a processor or blender. Set aside one third for salad.

2 boned loins of lamb (backstraps),
   trimmed of all fat & sinew
1–2 red onions, cut in eighths
8 wooden skewers, soaked in cold water
   for 30 minutes

Cut lamb into 2 cm slices. Then thread on skewers interspersed with wedges of onion. Barbecue, brushing with oil mix as you do so, until crusty on the outside and pink within.

½ cup crumbled feta cheese
½ cup Italian (flat leaf) parsley sprigs
1 punnet cherry tomatoes, halved
½ continental (telegraph) cucumber, sliced
   fairly thickly then halved
2–3 tbsp small black olives
tzatziki (see page 112)

Toss with reserved dressing to taste. Scatter on a platter and top with skewers. Serve tzatziki either on the side or sprinkled over the top.

Citrus juice in a marinade

will draw the red meat juices out if left too long, so either use in the above fashion as

a brushing sauce, or make sure that you only marinate briefly.

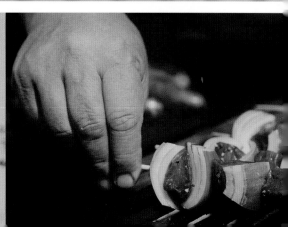

½ cup fresh herbs (parsley,
    mint & basil)
a clove of garlic, crushed
seasoning

2 lamb backstraps,
    trimmed of all fat & sinew
    (boned loin)
1-2 red onions, quartered

olive oil

Loin of lamb

. . . on barbecued potatoes with salsa rossa

2 red capsicums, roasted, peeled & diced
1–2 punnets small cherry tomatoes,
   quartered
2 tbsp red wine vinegar
4 tbsp olive oil
1 tbsp chopped fresh oregano
freshly ground salt & pepper

Toss and set aside to develop flavours.

---

12 baby potatoes, scrubbed well & cooked
   until just tender
2–3 boned loins of lamb (backstraps)
   trimmed of all fat & sinew

Halve potatoes and cook, cut side down first, on an oiled grill plate until crusty and brown all over. At the same time, cook lamb to desired degree, seasoning after sealed and then resting for a few minutes. Put potatoes on a platter, slice lamb and place on top and mound salsa on top of the lot.

. . . Tandoori mid-loin chops with mint raita

1 cup plain yoghurt
2 garlic cloves, crushed
1 tbsp garam masala
1 heaped tspn turmeric
1 heaped tspn paprika
½ tspn cayenne
2 cm piece fresh ginger, grated
2 tbsp lemon juice
freshly ground salt

Whisk.

12–18 mid-loin lamb chops

Toss in marinade and refrigerate for at least 2 hours.

---

raita (see page 112)

Remove chops from marinade, wipe off excess marinade and barbecue on a well-oiled grill to desired degree. Serve with raita on the side.

Lamb mini roasts

... smoked, with olive-oil dressed rocket

2 lamb mini roasts, trimmed of all fat
  & sinew
2 garlic cloves, cut into slivers
freshly ground salt & pepper
olive oil spray

Preheat kettle BBQ with indirect heat (see page 50). Make 8 or so small cuts in each roast and insert garlic slivers in them. Season well and spray with oil.

6 heaped cups hardwood sawdust
leaves from 1 bunch tarragon
1 head garlic, separated
1 tbsp coriander seeds
1 tbsp whole black peppercorns

Mix together, adding enough water so that it will form a ball when squeezed. When fire is ready, cover coals with 2 cm sawdust mix and adjust vents to ensure that coals are smouldering.

2–3 handfuls baby rocket
olive oil
balsamic vinegar

Put lamb in centre of rack, cover BBQ and after 20 minutes adjust vents to increase draft. Cook lamb to desired degree. Rest for 10 minutes and then slice. Serve with rocket, which has been dressed with oil and a little balsamic.

Lamb mini roasts

... with eggplant & capsicum peperonata

⅓ cup olive oil 1 heaped tbsp Dijon mustard a good splash of soy sauce freshly ground salt & pepper	Whisk well.
2 mini lamb roasts, well trimmed	Toss in lamb and leave for 30–40 minutes.
1 cup olive oil 1 large eggplant, cut in smallish cubes	Heat oil in a wok until almost smoking and then cook in 2 or 3 lots, until golden. Drain well.
1 large onion, chopped 2 garlic cloves, crushed	Poor off most of the oil and sauté until lightly coloured.
2 celery stalks, diced 1 red & 1 yellow capsicum, cored, seeded & diced	Add and toss for a few minutes.
2 cans chopped tomatoes a good splash of white wine 3 heaped tbsp chopped green olives 2 tbsp chopped parsley a splash of balsamic vinegar	Add and cook gently until thick and fragrant.

On a preheated, covered BBQ, cook lamb to desired degree. Then rest for 10 minutes. Serve either sliced or whole over peperonata (which can be warm or cold).

I normally advocate cooking lamb medium-rare but this cut is better cooked a little more than that (but still not well done) because the sinew that runs through it will not dissolve if too undercooked.

Leg of lamb

. . . roll your own souvlaki

1 cup olive oil 3 tbsp chopped fresh oregano 2 garlic cloves, crushed juice of 2–3 lemons freshly ground salt & pepper	Whisk.
1 butterflied leg of lamb, trimmed of excess fat	Pour marinade over and leave for 1 hour. Then cook to desired degree, covered, in preheated kettle BBQ (see page 50).
sauce tzatziki (see page 112)	Put in a bowl and place in the centre of an extra large platter.
¼–½ iceberg lettuce, washed & sliced 1 cup pitted black olives 6 ripe tomatoes, cored & cut in wedges ½–1 continental (telegraph) cucumber, sliced 2 medium red onions, sliced 1½ cups crumbled feta cheese 2–3 lemons, cut in wedges	Put in separate piles on a platter (leaving space for meat).
flat bread	When lamb is ready, rest for 10 minutes. Heat plenty of bread unoiled on BBQ. Then slice lamb, mound on the platter with salad, and serve bread alongside.

One of the biggest problems at any barbie

is that everyone, seemingly, wants their meat cooked differently. So, to make things easier, why not cook a whole joint such as the mustard-smeared rump on page 63) to rare or medium and then, if anyone wants it cooked more, just throw a thick slice back on the BBQ and cook it to the desired degree.

Leg of lamb

... steaks with a sweet 'n' spicy BBQ sauce & corn on the cob

4 cobs of corn, stripped of husk & silk	Blanch in salted boiling water for 5 minutes, drain well.
75 gm soft unsalted butter **a good squeeze of lemon juice** **1 tbsp chopped parsley**	Mix then put corn on squares of foil and smear generously with butter. Wrap up tightly and put on moderate part of BBQ.
1 cup tomato ketchup **½ cup raisins** **¼ cup red wine vinegar** **2 tbsp soy sauce** **2 tbsp honey** **a good slurp Tabasco**	In a small pot, combine and simmer for 5 minutes (this can be done on BBQ).
4–8 leg lamb steaks **freshly ground salt & pepper** **olive oil spray**	When corn is ready, spray, season and barbecue to desired degree, brushing generously with the sauce for the last 5 minutes or so. Serve with corn and extra sauce on the side.

When using a marinade, glaze or sauce

with a high sugar content, only brush it on the food in the last 10–15 minutes of

cooking otherwise it could burn.

The guts on the kettle BBQ

❀ Basically there are two methods of cooking in the kettle BBQ – direct and indirect. Indirect is more suitable for larger joints of meat, whole chickens and the like, and involves pushing the coal containers to the side and placing a foil tray in the centre to catch drips and prevent flare ups. With direct cooking, once coals are ready, remove from containers and scatter them over the grid.

❀ To light, place two firelighters in the base of each coal container, top with coals and light firelighters with long matches. Have lower vents wide open and don't put the cover on until coals are glowing and coated with a brownish ash (about 40–45minutes). Don't worry if, after the firelighters stop burning, the fire appears to go out – it hasn't and all will be well (for a hottish fire, I use 80–90 coals in total).

❀ Do keep in mind that, when cooking a large joint, every hour the coals need replenishing – just add a handful to each side.

❀ To raise and lower the temperature, open the vents (top and bottom) to increase and, obviously, close to decrease.

❀ Soaked woodchips add a wonderful flavour (in this instance the vents should be about one quarter open). Your BBQ shop will have a selection of different woods which need to be soaked overnight in cold water. Best for larger cuts and only a small handful is needed.

❀ In a similar vein, try adding to your coals apple peels, onion skins, apple tree or vine cuttings, or even sprigs of rosemary or stalks of lemongrass.

❀ And to keep everything moist, try putting a foil tray on top of the coals, half full of water, beer or wine (this works in similar vein to the Beer Can Chicken – see page 35).

❀ And just for your barbecue information, the Weber, which was the original kettle (and, to my mind, still the best) was created by metal worker George Stephen in 1952. He welded together two metal half spheres then added grates and legs. His friends, who found his creation amusing, christened it 'The Sputnik'. I wonder if any of them are laughing now.

Smoky aromas

of food being cooked over glowing coals still, to this day, excite my palate and invariably start my mouth watering.

Lamb offal

... a mixed grill of cutlets, kidneys, fry & various goodies

8 lamb cutlets, French trimmed	Batten out a little.
8 lamb kidneys **4 long rosemary stalks, most leaves removed**	Remove any outside membrane and halve lengthways. Then remove core with kitchen scissors and halve again crossways. Thread onto rosemary stalks.
4 large ripe tomatoes, cored & halved **4 large field mushrooms, peeled & stalks** **removed** **4 rindless bacon rashers** **olive oil spray** **1–2 lemons** **freshly ground salt & pepper**	Oil BBQ. Spray cutlets, kidneys and vegies with oil and season. Cook, along with bacon, squeezing lemon over meat as you do so. Keep both cutlets and kidneys pink.
4–8 thickish slices lamb's fry **chopped parsley** **lemon wedges**	When above is almost ready, oil lamb's fry and also cook until pink within. Pile the lot on a platter, sprinkle with parsley and serve with lemon wedges.

I believe I'm the only person

who has actually cooked on the hallowed turf of the Sydney Cricket Ground. When I whipped this up with spin maestro Stuart MacGill, he also taught me how to bowl a googly using a lemon – a skill which I'm sure will prove invaluable.

Veal cutlets

... with microwave blue cheese polenta

¼ cup olive oil juice of 1 lemon freshly ground salt & pepper 1 tbsp rosemary needles 4 veal cutlets, trimmed	Whisk oil, lemon and seasonings together and pour over veal. Leave for 30 minutes, turning 2 or 3 times.
3 cups water 1 cup polenta 1 tspn sea salt	Put in a microwave-proof bowl and cook, uncovered, at 100% for 6 minutes. Stir well, cover loosely with greaseproof paper and cook for a further 6 minutes.
2 dollops butter 150 gm soft blue cheese, diced freshly ground pepper	Add and mix in well. Cover tightly.
	When polenta is ready, barbecue veal, brushing with marinade as you do so. Serve with a large dollop of polenta.

I certainly don't advocate serving veal rare

but a touch of pink is necessary to ensure that it is not dry.

Veal cutlets

... spice-rubbed with a grilled fennel, tomato & red onion salad

2 garlic cloves, crushed 2 tbsp seeded mustard 2 tbsp olive oil 1 tbsp smoked paprika ½ cup finely chopped fresh sage, rosemary & thyme freshly ground salt	Mix together.
4 veal cutlets, trimmed	Rub mix into veal and set aside to develop flavours. (Refrigerate any leftover mix.)
3 small fennel bulbs, cored & cut into thinnish wedges 2 red onions, cut into thinnish wedges olive oil spray freshly ground salt & pepper	Spray and season vegetables. Barbecue over a moderate heat until tender and slightly charred.
3 ripe tomatoes, cored & quartered	When above vegies are almost ready, oil and season tomatoes and add.
olive oil balsamic vinegar	Put vegetables in a bowl and toss with oil and vinegar to taste.
olive oil spray	Spray veal, barbecue and serve on a mound of salad.

but if you don't happen to have a jar in your pantry just use the normal variety.

Porterhouse or rump steaks

SERVES
6–8

... minute steak with 3 herb & garlic chimichurri

1 cup Italian (flat leaf) parsley leaves
1 cup coriander leaves
½ cup mint leaves
6 garlic cloves, chopped
3 anchovies
½ tspn sambal oelek
freshly ground salt & pepper
1 cup olive oil
a good splash of red wine vinegar

Blend and set aside to develop flavours.

6–8 x 120 gm steaks, trimmed of all
    fat & sinew

Batten out a little and brush both sides with plenty of the above. Barbecue to the desired degree, brushing with more chimichurri as you do so. To serve, sprinkle generously with more sauce.

SERVES
4

... with Kick Arse sauce & lemony smashed potatoes

8–12 baby potatoes, scrubbed

Boil in lightly salted water until tender. Drain, cover and keep hot.

---

4 x 220 gm steaks, trimmed well
BBQ sauce (either my Kick Arse or Big Tex's
    version on page 113)

When spuds are ready, barbecue steaks to desired degree, brushing generously with sauce towards the end.

¼ cup olive oil
juice of 1 lemon
1 heaped tspn Dijon mustard
freshly ground salt & pepper

Mix.

Crush potatoes roughly with a fork, adding oil mixture and mound on plates or a platter. Top with steaks and serve extra sauce on the side.

Porterhouse or rump steaks

... peppered in a steak sandwich with Dijon mustard aioli

4 x 150 gm steaks, trimmed of all fat & sinew
olive oil
freshly ground salt & pepper
1 large onion, thickly sliced

Preheat BBQ. Season steaks generously with pepper. Then cook steaks to desired degree, along with onion on an oiled grill. Season with salt once sealed.

½ cup mayonnaise
3 tbsp sour cream
2 garlic cloves, crushed
1 heaped tbsp Dijon mustard

Whisk together.

8 thick slices country-style bread
tomato chutney, bought or homemade
   (see page 116) or relish
1 handful baby rocket leaves

Brush bread lightly with oil and grill. Then put aioli on 4 pieces, top with onion, beef, chutney and rocket. Top with other slices of bread.

Salt draws out the juices from a steak

so only ever add it after you have sealed your steak (it doesn't matter so much in a marinade).

T-bone steaks

... with Café de Paris butter

6–8 thick T-bone steaks
olive oil spray
freshly ground salt & pepper

Spray steaks generously with oil and barbecue over a fairly high heat to desired degree (seasoning once sealed). Rest for 5 minutes.

Café de Paris butter (see page 115)
jacket potatoes (see page 82)

Serve with thick slices of the butter on top and jacket potatoes on the side.

... bistecca alla fiorentina

Traditionally this steak is served crusty on the outside and rare within – also the most common accompaniment is a pile of steamed or sautéed spinach.

100 gm soft unsalted butter
1 heaped tbsp chopped parsley
zest & juice of 1 lemon

Mix well.

4 x 300 gm T-bone steaks
olive oil
freshly ground salt & pepper
2 garlic cloves, halved

Brush steaks generously with oil, add a generous grinding of pepper and throw onto an oiled BBQ. Once sealed, turn, season with salt and rub garlic cloves, flesh side down, vigorously along bone. Cook to desired degree and serve with a good dollop of the butter.

How to cook the perfect steak

- The most important factor is the quality of the meat itself. Buy the best and don't ever, ever buy that which the butcher deems to be perfect for the barbie (this is normally a throwback to the days when steaks were invariably incinerated which therefore meant the quality didn't really matter).

- Apart from quality, the other major problem is that the steaks are cut too thin and are often also cut unevenly. What is required is a steak which is at least 2 cm thick and is of an even thickness from one end to the other.

- Always pull your steak out of the refrigerator at least 30 minutes before you plan to barbecue it. This brings it up to room temperature which ensures it will cook more quickly and evenly.

- Trim most, if not all of the fat from it (if leaving some on, make a few nicks to stop it curling).

- Preheat the BBQ, spray the steak with oil and start it on a well-oiled spot over high heat. When crusty on one side, turn over and move to a fresh part of the grill to ensure the intensity of the heat is still there. Season once sealed (salt draws the juices out of raw meat) and, depending on how you like it cooked, move it to a more moderate part of the grill once well sealed.

- And last, but certainly not least, don't play with the blessed thing. I know it looks like you know what you're doing when you are continually prodding, poking and turning, but a steak only needs to be turned a few times at most and should not be prodded and poked, particularly with BBQ forks or knives, as this will only release the essential juices.

Fillet of beef

... in a spicy Cuban salad

½ cup olive oil
zest of 1 lime
juice of 2 limes
2 cloves garlic, crushed
1 heaped tspn sambal oelek
2 tbsp each chopped parsley & coriander
freshly ground salt

Whisk and set two thirds aside.

2 x 200 gm fillet steaks, trimmed of all
    fat & sinew

Add to the one third of above dressing, toss well and leave for 30 minutes.

4 wooden skewers, soaked in cold water
    for 30 minutes
2 red onions, thickly sliced
freshly ground pepper

Put onion slices on skewers, oil and season steak and onions generously and barbecue both. When cooked to desired degree, rest beef for 5 minutes.

4 radishes, cut in wedges
1 red capsicum, finely sliced
4 spring (green) onions, in 2–3 cm lengths
10 cherry tomatoes, halved
2 chillies, finely sliced
handful inner cos leaves

Cube beef and add along with onions and dressing to taste. Serve in a large bowl.

Like most Cuban food

this should be tart, spicy and full of flavour. And skewering the onions ensures that while the outsides will be charred, the insides will still be crisp and crunchy.

Fillet of beef

. . . whole with barbecued field mushrooms & garlic butter

**1 whole fillet of beef, trimmed of all
fat & sinew**
olive oil spray
freshly ground salt & pepper

Fold tail underneath and, with kitchen string, tie at 3–4 cm intervals. Spray with oil, season and barbecue to desired degree. (Start off on hot part of grill to seal well, then move to more moderate part.) When ready, rest for 5 minutes.

**12–18 large flat field mushrooms, peeled
& stalks discarded**

At the same time, generously oil and season mushrooms and throw on grill.

garlic butter (see page 115)

Slice beef, put on a platter with mushrooms and top the lot with thick slices of garlic butter and any meat juices poured over.

. . . steak, egg, chips & me mum's tomato sauce

A good old-fashioned favourite.

potato shells (see page 104)
freshly ground salt

Throw on the BBQ and cook until crisp. Season.

**4 x 200 gm fillet steaks, trimmed of all
fat & sinew**
olive oil spray
freshly ground salt & pepper
4 large eggs

Spray steaks with oil and cook over a high heat to the desired degree, seasoning when sealed. Rest for 5 minutes. Cook eggs in egg rings on a well-oiled grill plate.

homemade tomato sauce (see page 113)

Put steaks on plates, top with eggs, mound chips on the side and serve with a good dollop of sauce.

Joints of beef

... mustard-smeared rump with a charred onion salad

olive oil spray
6–8 large brown onions, skin on
   & halved crossways
freshly ground salt & pepper

Preheat kettle BBQ with indirect heat (see page 50). Spray cut sides of onions with oil, season and place flesh side down around edges of BBQ. Cover and cook, turning and spraying every now and then.

1 whole beef rump, trimmed well
seeded mustard

Season top side of beef and smear generously with mustard. Put in centre of BBQ over a drip tray (fat down) and cook, covered, to desired degree. Remove and rest for 10 minutes before slicing.

extra virgin olive oil
red wine vinegar
freshly ground salt & pepper
chopped parsley

To make salad, slip onions from skin and dress to taste with oil, vinegar, seasonings and parsley.

... vodka-perfumed standing rib roast

The vodka breaks down the fat a little and, talking about fat, ask your butcher to trim the joint well and also tie it with butcher's string at regular intervals.

1 x 3½–4 kilo standing rib roast, French
   trimmed
vodka
freshly ground pepper & salt
6–8 bay leaves
a few handfuls of woodchips soaked in
   water overnight

Preheat kettle BBQ with indirect heat (see page 50) with large drip tray in centre. Massage beef all over with a generous amount of vodka and season well. Make small cuts at regular intervals and insert bay leaves. Put roast in centre of BBQ, ensuring that none of it is over coals. Add a handful of soaked woodchips to both piles of coals and cover. Cook to desired degree (about 1¼ hours for medium-rare) with vents a quarter of the way open. When ready, cover loosely with foil and rest for 15–20 minutes before carving.

Kangaroo

... skewered with Indian flavours & a spiced onion relish

½ cup coconut cream
1 heaped tbsp medium-hot Indian
   curry paste
a good splash of soy sauce
1 cm piece of ginger, grated
2 garlic cloves, crushed
juice of 1–2 limes

Whisk together.

2–3 kangaroo fillets, trimmed of all
   fat & sinew

Cut in 1½ cm slices. Toss in marinade and leave for an hour or so.

---

2 large red onions, finely sliced
2 tspn paprika
1 tspn cayenne
juice of 1–2 limes
3 tbsp chopped coriander
freshly ground salt & pepper

While kangaroo is marinating, mix together and massage with your fingers for a few minutes. Set aside to develop flavours.

---

8 wooden skewers soaked in cold water
   for 30 minutes
lime wedges

Thread roo on skewers and barbecue quickly over a high heat, brushing with marinade as you do so. Scatter onion relish over plates or a platter, top with skewers and serve with lime wedges.

Kangaroo is low in fat

therefore it shouldn't be overcooked – so at the very most medium-rare (otherwise it will be tough and dry).

Kangaroo

... seared, Moroccan lemon sauce & rice cooker pilaf

olive oil 1 onion, chopped 2 garlic cloves, crushed	Heat a little oil and sauté in a heavy-bottomed pot until soft.
1 tspn paprika 1 tspn cumin seeds 2 cinnamon sticks a good grinding of black pepper	Add and toss for a minute or two.
3 cups chicken stock (bought is fine) juice of 1–2 lemons	Add and reduce until thickish.
¼ cup chopped coriander	Add and keep warm.
2 cups basmati rice	Run under cold water until water runs clear, then drain.
olive oil spray ½ onion, finely chopped 3 baby carrots, finely diced ½ celery stalk, finely diced	Start rice cooker, spray oil on base and sauté vegetables. Add rice.
2½ cups chicken stock (bought is fine) ½ tspn cumin a good pinch of salt	Add, mix well and cover. Start machine again and cook until machine turns to warming cycle.
½ tspn grated lemon zest 4 tbsp butter 4 tbsp chopped fresh parsley	Add, stir, cover again and leave for 10 minutes. Fluff with a fork.
4 kangaroo fillets, trimmed of all fat & sinew	Cook on an oiled BBQ over a high heat until crusty on the outside yet still rare within. Rest for 5 minutes, then slice and serve on rice with sauce over the top.

Kangaroo

. . . on a Greek salad with pita & garlic yoghurt

2 tbsp chopped fresh oregano 4 tbsp olive oil juice of 1 lemon 1 garlic clove, crushed freshly ground salt & pepper	Whisk together.
1 punnet cherry tomatoes, halved ½–1 red onion, sliced ½ continental (telegraph) cucumber, halved lengthwise & sliced ¼ cup Italian (flat leaf) parsley sprigs ½ cup feta cheese, crumbled	Add to above and toss well.
2–3 kangaroo fillets, trimmed of all fat & sinew olive oil spray 1 lemon	Spray roo with oil, season and barbecue, squeezing lemon juice over as you do so. Cook until crusty on the outside but rareish within. Remove and rest for 5 minutes.
4–6 medium pita tzatziki (see page 112)	While meat is resting, throw pita on the BBQ and then put on plates and mound with salad. Slice roo and put on top along with any juices and a sprinkling of tzatziki.

The kangaroo is not an endangered species

(in fact it is culled in many parts of Australia). So relax and enjoy this delicious rich meat, which just happens to be very low in cholesterol to boot.

Mince

... bo la lot (minced beef in betel leaves)

peanut oil ½ red onion, finely chopped 2 garlic cloves, crushed 2 chillies, seeded & finely sliced 1–2 lemongrass stalks, grated	Heat a little oil in a wok or pan and sauté vegetables.
350 gm minced beef 1½ tbsp Asian fish sauce 1 tbsp shaved palm sugar freshly ground salt & pepper	Put in a bowl, add vegies and mix thoroughly.
25–30 large betel leaves, well washed 8–12 wooden skewers, soaked in cold water for 30 minutes	Put a heaped teaspoon or so of mince in centre of betel leaf and roll up, folding sides in first. Lay 3 or 4 alongside each other on a bench and put 1 or 2 wooden skewers through them crossways.
¼ cup peanut oil 3 spring (green) onions, green part only, finely sliced freshly ground salt a pinch of shaved palm sugar	Heat oil in a pot. Turn off, add sugar and salt and stir to dissolve. Then add spring onion. Brush stuffed leaves with oil and barbecue, brushing with more oil as you do so. Serve with extra oil mix on the side.

A delicious Vietnamese dish

which is normally served as a starter. And betel leaves are available in many Asian groceries (particularly those in Vietnamese areas).

Weird but wonderful BBQ tales

I once had a great mate Fred, who was actually a rather good cook. Unfortunately he was also in the habit of drinking rather heavily from the moment he began preparing for the big event. After a few near disasters (falling into the pool, knocking over the kettle barbie, falling asleep under the tree before lunch etc.) Fred was barred by his wife from inviting anyone to his Sunday feasts. And the moral of this tale? Try to keep away from that slab of beer or case of chardonnay until after your chores are done!

A scientific study recently found that mosquitoes are more attracted to certain people (strangely enough, it was felt that it was because their blood was sweeter). So, at the next barbie, ask around until you find someone that is always being bitten by the bloody things – and stick to them like glue.

Amazingly, not everyone loves the barbie. One Bavarian woman recently took her neighbour to court to stop her complaining of the BBQ smells wafting over her fence. The Bavarian Supreme Court sympathised with her and instructed the neighbour that only five barbies were permitted each year – ouch!

I may have told you this story before about the I Spit On Your Gravy barbecue. The Gravies (a rather badly behaved band from the 70s and 80s) used to 'borrow' a supermarket shopping trolley, prop it on its side, light a fire on the bottom and cook their steaks on the top. According to my mate Filthy Phil, a member of the aforementioned band, the food was either burnt or raw, but due to a high degree of inebriation, no one appeared to notice.

In a recent British study, 59% of women surveyed said that their partner's love of grilling was because they thought it made them look more macho and rugged. And almost all of them felt that it was because it gave them a legitimate excuse to play with fire.

Mince

... beetroot, beef & sweet chilli burgers

vegetable oil **1 onion, chopped** **2 rindless bacon rashers, diced**	Heat oil in a pan and gently sauté. Put in a bowl.
4 slices beetroot, diced **a little beetroot juice** **500 gm lean minced beef** **1 egg** **12 capers, chopped** **2 tbsp sweet chilli sauce** **3 tbsp chopped coriander**	Add and mix well. Form into burger patties using pastry cutters or egg rings. Cook on an oiled BBQ grill plate.
4–6 English muffins, halved **mayonnaise** **4–6 cos lettuce leaves** **Vietnamese mint** **sweet chilli sauce**	When burgers are almost ready, cook muffins on grill. Put muffin bottoms on bench and top with mayonnaise, lettuce, mint sprigs, meat patties, a generous slurp of sweet chilli sauce and finally the muffin tops.

An unusual-sounding combination

that actually works brilliantly – particularly if, like me, you are a lover of beetroot. (I feel

that, in a similar vein to Vegemite, it's almost un-Australian to not like beetroot.)

Mince

... Sicilian meatball shish kebab

500 gm minced lamb
1 large egg
¼ cup grated pecorino cheese
¼ cup hot salami, diced
2 tbsp chopped parsley
½ cup dried breadcrumbs
2 garlic cloves, crushed
1 heaped tspn sambal oelek
freshly ground salt & pepper

Mix well and roll into smallish meatballs (about the size of a walnut). Refrigerate for at least 30 minutes.

wooden skewers, soaked in cold water
for 30 minutes
½ loaf sourdough bread, cut in 2 cm cubes
fresh sage leaves

Skewer meatballs, alternating with bread and sage leaves.

olive oil spray
2–3 lemons

Spray meatballs generously and barbecue on an oiled grill, squeezing with lemon juice as you do so.

3–4 dozen green beans, topped & tailed
olive oil
balsamic vinegar
lemon wedges

Blanch green beans until crisp-tender in lots of lightly salted boiling water (this can be done beforehand). Drain well and toss with oil and balsamic to taste. Scatter on a platter, top with shish kebabs and serve with lemon wedges on the side. (Beans can be served warm or at room temperature.)

Mince

... Indian koftas in pita

vegetable oil
½ onion, finely chopped
2 garlic cloves, crushed
2 tbsp medium-hot Indian curry paste

Heat oil in a pan and sauté vegetables until soft. Then throw in paste and toss for a few seconds.

250 gm lean minced veal
150 gm minced pork
2 tbsp Indian lime pickles, chopped
1–2 tbsp yoghurt
3 tbsp chopped coriander
freshly ground salt & pepper

Put in a bowl with above and mix well. Form into meatballs about 2½ cm across and then flatten slightly.

4–6 pieces pita bread
12 slices tomato
12 slices continental (telegraph) cucumber
3–4 cos lettuce leaves, sliced
raita (see page 112)

Cook koftas on a preheated, oiled BBQ plate. When ready, heat pita, slice off one edge and stuff with koftas, tomato, cucumber, lettuce and a generous sprinkling of raita.

Always clean your barbie after cooking

with a stiff brush and an oiled cloth. And do it while it's still hot – it's a lot easier.

Mince

... the good old-fashioned Huey burger

vegetable oil **1 onion, chopped** **2 garlic cloves, crushed**	Heat a little oil in a pan and sauté vegetables until soft. Put in a bowl.
750 gm minced beef **¼ cup tomato chutney** **2 eggs, lightly beaten** **2 tbsp Worcestershire sauce** **freshly ground salt & pepper**	Add to bowl, mix well and form into patties.
grated tasty cheese **1–2 onions, peeled & thickly sliced**	Oil BBQ grill plate and cook patties and onions. When patties are almost ready, press cheese into top. Allow cheese to melt a little, then remove and keep warm.
8 rindless bacon rashers **8 burger buns, halved**	Cook bacon and burger buns on grill plate.
mayonnaise **crisp lettuce (cos or iceberg)** **3–4 large tomatoes, thickly sliced** **sliced beetroot** **tomato chutney (bought or homemade (see page 116) or tomato sauce**	Smear bun bottoms with mayonnaise, top with lettuce, tomato, beetroot, onion, bacon, burger, egg and chutney. Top with upper half of buns.

A tip from American food guru

The late James Beard always placed a couple of small ice cubes into the middle

of a burger patty just before cooking to keep it moist.

Mince

. . . Persian kebabs with minted cucumber salad

600 gm lamb mince juice of 1–2 limes 3 garlic cloves, crushed 1 heaped tspn each ground cumin, coriander & paprika 1 heaped tspn sambal oelek 2 tbsp Indian mango chutney	Mix well and refrigerate for 45 minutes.
12 wooden skewers, soaked in cold water for 30 minutes	With wet hands, form along skewers in a sausage shape.
3–4 limes, halved olive oil	Put lime halves on grill plate, cut side down, and cook until they caramelise. When almost ready, brush kebabs with oil and cook brushing and turning frequently (and carefully).
1 large continental (telegraph) cucumber, sliced on the diagonal & halved 8 mint leaves, sliced ½ cup plain yoghurt 6 medium pita	Mix cucumber, mint and yoghurt together. Grill pita and top with salad and kebabs. Serve with grilled lime on the side.

Caramelising the limes

gives them a wonderful smoky flavour – great squeezed over almost any barbecued food.

Sausages

. . . in the Huey dog

8 thick pork sausages	Cook in simmering water until firmish when squeezed. Drain and set aside.
2 tbsp olive oil **3 large onions, sliced** **grated tasty cheese**	Heat oil in a pan and gently sauté onions until lightly caramelised. Then make a fairly deep cut in the sausage from end to end (on the side that curls up) and stuff with onion and then cheese. Place on the BBQ grid between slats until cheese begins to melt (you may need to cover).
2 French sticks **tomato sauce** **mustard in squeezy bottle**	If bread is fresh, use as is. If not, heat in oven or on BBQ. Cut bread crossways into lengths about the same size as the sausages. Cut almost through from the top down. Smear with tomato sauce (adding any leftover onion). Put sausages in and squeeze mustard over the top in the traditional crossways pattern.

I came up with this rather silly hot dog

when I went to the footy and had a dreadful little number with stale buns and ordinary,

to say the least, frankfurters. Even the tomato sauce and mustard were of inferior quality.

Sausages

... with smoky Boston baked beans

3 cups cannellini beans	Soak overnight in cold water. Then drain.
olive oil **1 large onion, chopped**	Preheat kettle BBQ (see page 50). Heat a little oil in a heavy-bottomed pot on the BBQ and sauté onion.
1 cup dry white wine **2 cups canned tomato puree** **1 cup BBQ sauce (my Kick-Arse Sauce** **would be great)** **2 level tbsp brown sugar** **1 heaped tbsp molasses** **1 heaped tbsp Dijon mustard** **plenty of freshly ground pepper** **rock salt**	Add along with beans and mix well. Put lid on BBQ and cook for 1–1½ hours until tender (adding water as needed).
12–16 thick sausages of any variety	Blanch in simmering water until just firm when squeezed. Drain well and set aside until needed.
	When beans are ready, barbecue sausages until golden. Put beans on plates or a platter, and top with bangers.

You can cook the beans on the stove

but the smoky flavour from the kettle BBQ is wonderful. And, if you must, you can just make the sauce, adding well-drained and rinsed canned beans towards the end.

Rack of pork

... with a herb & mustard persillade

**1 x 6 cutlet pork rack, French trimmed
olive oil spray
freshly ground salt & pepper**

Preheat kettle BBQ with indirect heat and drip tray (see page 50). Trim skin and most of the fat from pork, oil and season. Then place over tray, cover and cook for 35–40 minutes.

**¾ cup dried breadcrumbs
2 garlic cloves, crushed
3 tbsp chopped parsley
4 tbsp melted butter**

Mix with enough butter to make slightly moist.

Dijon mustard

Remove pork, brush generously with mustard and press persillade firmly on top. Return to BBQ and cook for another 15 minutes or so. (Spray persillade crust with a little oil if it is drying out.)

Barbecued pears would go beautifully with this

Just cut pears lengthways (core and all), brush with oil and cook briefly over the hot part of the grill – and, by the way, this is the perfect time to use an instant-read thermometer.

Pork cutlets or chops

... with a peachy keen BBQ sauce

olive oil ½ onion, chopped 1 heaped tspn grated fresh ginger 1 garlic clove, crushed	Heat a little oil in a small pot on the BBQ and sauté vegies until soft.
4 canned peaches, diced 2 cups tomato ketchup ½ cup peach jam 1 tbsp red wine vinegar	Add, move to the side of the BBQ and simmer for 20 minutes. Keep warm.
6–8 thick pork cutlets or chops	Oil BBQ and cook pork over a moderate heat, brushing with sauce towards the end. Serve with extra sauce on the side.

... oregano-marinated 'panuntella'

Panuntella literally means greased bread.

1 cup olive oil 2 garlic cloves, crushed 3 tbsp chopped fresh oregano juice of 1 lemon freshly ground salt & pepper	Preheat kettle BBQ with indirect heat and a large drip tray (see page 50). Then whisk marinade ingredients.
4–6 thick pork chops	Put in marinade and leave for 30 minutes or so.
4–6 thick slices country-style bread	Put the bread in the drip tray and sprinkle with a little marinade. Return to lower grid. Barbecue pork chops on rack above drip tray, brushing generously with marinade as you do so. When pork is ready, put bread on plates, top with chops and pour any juices from the drip tray over the top. (You may need to turn the bread over halfway through cooking.)

A brine for pork

... to ensure that it is juicy & flavoursome

Over 15 years ago I dined at Jeremiah Tower's wonderful San Francisco restaurant, Stars, and I can still taste the brilliant thick double pork chop which had been barbecued yet was still succulent & juicy (a cut this thick tends to dry out when cooked over high heat).

Well, now all is revealed. In his latest book, *Jeremiah Tower Cooks*, he lets us into his secret – a dunk in a simple brine which almost guarantees moist juicy meat (the other 'secret' is not to overcook it). So next time you are cooking pork, any cut, throw it in this brine and I promise you, you will be amazed by the result (different cuts need different times in the brine i.e. leg of pork – 48 hours, pork chops – 3 or 4 hours).

5 litres water
1 cup rock or sea salt
½ cup sugar
1 head garlic, smashed
1 tbsp juniper berries, crushed
6 sprigs fresh thyme
6 bay leaves, torn
4 dried red chillies, chopped
½ cup chopped fresh parsley

Heat water, add everything and stir until salt and sugar dissolve. Chill before using. The brine can be reused but needs to be strained after each use (and also must be kept in the fridge at all times). And keep in mind that the brine needs to completely cover the marinating pork.

The perfect way

to entertain a group of
friends on a hot sunny day
is an outdoor barbecue.

½ cup olive oil
a good squeeze of lemon
½ cup fresh herbs (parsley,
mint & basil)
a clove of garlic, crushed
seasoning

Pork spare ribs

... Texas-style with jacket potatoes

4–8 jacket potatoes, scrubbed well	Preheat kettle BBQ with direct heat (see page 50). Then wrap potatoes individually in foil and put around outside of BBQ grill.
4 slabs baby back ribs **Big Tex's BBQ sauce (see page 113)**	After potatoes have been cooking for 15 minutes, brush ribs generously with sauce and barbecue for 30–40 minutes, brushing and turning regularly.
sour cream **chopped chives**	When ribs and potatoes are ready, unwrap and cut a cross in top of spuds then add a dollop of sour cream and a sprinkling of chives. Serve alongside ribs with any extra rib sauce on the side.

In the Southern states of America

barbecuing is more of a religion than a pastime, barbecue sauces are a family secret passed down from generation to generation and the barbie itself often takes up more room than the house. Which is a bit of a contrast to the good old Aussie number that is purely a social event and which will really only fail if the beer runs out or the missus has forgotten to buy enough tomato sauce.

Pork spare ribs

... east meets west with a pile of Thai slaw

1 large onion, finely chopped	Whisk together.
2 garlic cloves, crushed	
1 tbsp grated fresh ginger	
4 tbsp soy sauce	
4 tbsp Chinese black vinegar	
4 tbsp Chinese rice wine	
4 tbsp water	
2 tbsp sambal oelek	
4 tbsp tomato puree	
4 tbsp honey	
freshly ground salt & pepper	

6–8 slabs baby back ribs	Preheat kettle BBQ with direct heat (see page 50). Brush ribs generously with sauce and barbecue, covered, until tender, brushing regularly with sauce.

Thai slaw (see page 98)	Either serve slabs whole or cut into individual ribs with slaw on the side.

This is true finger food

so plenty of napkins and fingerbowls are essential. And I am sure we've all heard at least one wag, when the fingerbowls arrive, attempt to encourage us to drink the 'lemon soup'. But I did have one restaurant patron drink the stuff before complaining to the waiter about it's lack of flavour – and sadly, I think he was actually serious.

Cheese

. . . 3 varieties on a pizza with garlic oil & grilled tomatoes

2½ tspn dry yeast 1 cup warm water a pinch of sugar	Combine in a bowl. Stand for about 5 minutes until foaming.
3 tbsp rye flour 2 tspn sea salt olive oil 2–3 cups strong bread flour	Add rye flour, salt and 1 tbsp olive oil. Mix and gradually add 2 cups of flour (should be fairly stiff). Knead on a well floured bench until smooth and elastic, adding more flour if sticky. Put in a lightly oiled bowl, cover and leave in a warm spot until doubled in size (1½–2 hours). Punch down, knead lightly and leave until doubled again.
½ cup olive oil 1 garlic clove, crushed	Combine oil and garlic. Punch dough down, divide into 4 and roll out thinly. Drape, 1 or 2 at a time, on preheated BBQ and when it begins to puff, turn over and brush with flavoured oil.
6–8 ripe red tomatoes, cored & thickly sliced 4–6 bocconcini, finely sliced 1 cup grated gruyere ½ cup grated Italian parmesan	Briefly cook tomatoes on grill plate. Put on pizza, along with bocconcini, and top with gruyere and parmesan. Cook, covered, on moderate part of BBQ until cheese has melted. Drizzle with a little more garlic oil.
1 handful baby rocket	Toss with a little oil and scatter over the top.

The top needs to be on for the final cooking

but if using a normal barbie, once you have added the tomato and cheeses, cover with a wok lid or a large foil tray.

Barbecued flat bread

...with various toppings

Certainly not quite as classy as my BBQ Pizza (see page 84) but delicious nonetheless.
And the toppings – well I leave those up to your imagination although here are a few of my
suggestions just to get you started. (Oh, and I almost forgot, oil both sides of the bread,
grill one side then turn over and add a thin layer of topping. Move to moderate part of BBQ,
cover and cook until hot.)

- a sprinkling of rosemary needles & sea salt flakes

- sauté onions with a splash of balsamic, then when ready, pile on barbecued flat bread,
top with sliced smoked salmon and a sprinkling of sour cream

- a good tomato-based pasta sauce topped with sliced
salami and pitted olives

- the classic tomato, bocconcini & basil salad

- sliced prosciutto, cherry tomatoes & grated gruyere

- finely sliced barbecued lamb on eggplant & capsicum peperonata (see page 46)

- prosciutto & sliced fresh figs (add the figs at the last moment to just heat through)

Cheese

... goat's cheese stuffed eggplant

½ cup olive oil 1 tbsp honey juice of 1 lemon freshly ground salt & pepper 1 garlic clove, crushed	Whisk together.
2 large eggplants, sliced evenly lengthways (½ cm thick)	Brush generously with oil mix and barbecue, brushing regularly with oil mix until golden and tender.
sundried tomato pesto, bought 1–2 soft goat's cheeses 8 wooden skewers, soaked in cold water for 30 minutes	Smear each slice with a little pesto, top with a dollop of cheese and roll up. Place 3 on a bench alongside each other and push 2 skewers through crossways. Repeat process.
16 cherry tomatoes, quartered ¼ continental (telegraph) cucumber, sliced & quartered 12 black olives, pitted & sliced 1 small handful frissee lettuce	Toss with olive oil mix to taste and scatter on plates or platter.
	Barbecue eggplant rolls, brushing with oil mix as you do so, and put on salad.

Cheese

... spinach & goat's cheese quesadillas

olive oil ½ onion, finely chopped 2 chillies, seeded & finely sliced 1 garlic clove, crushed	Heat a little oil in a wok or pan and sauté vegetables.
2 handfuls baby spinach leaves, well washed freshly ground salt & pepper	Add to pan and toss briefly until wilted. Put in a colander to drain. Then squeeze out any excess moisture and chop coarsely.
250 gm soft goat's cheese 8 flour tortillas 2–3 tbsp sour cream 50–100 gm tasty cheese, grated	Mix goat's cheese with sour cream. Lay 4 tortillas on a bench and spread with goat's cheese (leaving an edge), top with spinach mix and a little tasty cheese. Then wet edge with water and firmly press other tortillas on top (don't overstuff).
3 large ripe tomatoes, diced ½ red capsicum, cored, seeded & finely diced ½ red onion, finely chopped juice of 1–2 limes freshly ground salt & pepper	Mix together.
sour cream	Cook quesadillas on an oiled BBQ grill plate until golden on each side. Then serve topped with salsa and a dollop of sour cream.

Experiment with different fillings

but do remember – don't get carried away with the amount of stuffing. And the flour tortillas

– these are also sometimes called burritos and are available in supermarkets everywhere.

Salad corner

Salads certainly play an important role at any BBQ, but not just any old salads. Forget those tired, limp little numbers that always appear to have sat out in the sun far too long. Instead think fresh zingy versions using hardier ingredients which enable them to last without deterioration for a longer period of time. And here are a few of my favourites just to get you started:

- Bar room slaw – finely sliced cabbage and red onion with grated carrot and a sauce made from aioli (see page 114), to which hot water has been added to make it of a dressing consistency.

- Barbecue corn on the cob until charred. Cut off kernels and toss with sliced radicchio and witloof and your favourite vinaigrette to which you have added chopped anchovies.

- Whiz up $1/2$ cup olive oil, a good squeeze of lemon juice, a garlic clove, seasonings and $1/2$ cup parsley, mint and basil leaves. Then toss tomato wedges, sliced onion, pitted olives, frisee lettuce and plenty of crumbled feta along with the dressing to taste.

- For a pasta or rice salad (with plenty of crispy, crunchy vegies), try this dressing. Mix 2 tbsp sherry vinegar, juice of 1 lemon, 4 tbsp seeded mustard, 1 crushed garlic clove, $1/2$ cup olive oil, $1/2$ cup freshly grated parmesan and 1 tbsp sour cream.

- One of my favourites includes seeded, cubed watermelon, sliced red onion, crumbled feta and sliced black olives along with fresh herb leaves and a dressing made from olive oil, lemon juice and harissa (see page 111).

- Make an American-style ranch dressing which is great over cos lettuce leaves along with some crispy bacon. Mix 4 tbsp mayo, 2 tbsp each buttermilk and sour cream, 3 tbsp freshly grated parmesan, 2 chopped anchovies and a splash each of Tabasco and Worcester.

- Blanch plenty of green beans and toss with pesto (bought or homemade) and fresh parmesan shavings or sliced semi-dried tomatoes along with some of their oil.

- And let us not forget crunchy iceberg lettuce. Simply clean, core and cut into wedges. Then dress with a blue cheese dressing made by whisking together 1 cup mayonnaise, $1/2$ cup plain yoghurt, $1/4$ cup buttermilk, 3 tbsp white vinegar, seasonings and $1/2$–$3/4$ cup crumbled blue cheese.

Mixed vegies

... escalivados in the Spanish style

3 medium brown onions, skin on
olive oil spray
freshly ground salt & pepper

Cut onions in half crossways, spray with oil and season generously. Cook, cut side down first, on the moderate part of BBQ, turning and spraying every now and then until tender when pierced with a sharp knife. Peel separate layers and pile on a platter.

2 large eggplants, thickly sliced
6 large flat mushrooms, peeled
6 ripe tomatoes, cored & halved

Oil and season eggplants and mushrooms and barbecue until charred and tender, spraying and turning regularly. When almost ready, repeat process with tomatoes. Add to platter in separate piles.

2 red capsicums, roasted & cut in 4
  (see page 110)
2 yellow capsicums, roasted and cut in 4
  (see page 110)

Leaving any juices behind, toss briefly on BBQ then place on platter.

½ cup olive oil
good splash of sherry vinegar
1 heaped tspn capers
2 tbsp chopped parsley

Whisk along with any capsicum juices and sprinkle over the top. Serve with plenty of crusty bread.

Mixed vegies

... in foil packets

In the States they have a delightful name for such packets which they roast in the coals. They call them 'hobo packs' so named because the hobos (tramps) during the Great Depression used to wrap any food in newspaper and throw it on the coals to cook (this negated the hassle of carrying cooking utensils around).

12 baby carrots, peeled
2 corn cobs, blanched & thickly sliced
12 button mushrooms, wiped clean
16–20 sugar snap peas, topped & tailed
2 baby bok choy, cleaned & halved
   lengthways
soy sauce or olive oil

Share vegies amongst 4 large squares of heavy-duty foil. Sprinkle with soy or olive oil (season if using oil), fold up and crimp edges. Put on a preheated BBQ and cook until vegies are tender.

... an Italian vegie burger

2 medium zucchinis, sliced
2 red capsicums, cored, seeded & cut
   in even pieces
1 medium eggplant, halved lengthways
   & then sliced in half moons
12 medium flat mushrooms, peeled
olive oil
freshly ground salt & pepper

Oil and season vegetables and barbecue until tender and lightly charred. Remove to a bowl.

6–8 burger buns, halved
2–3 large ripe tomatoes, cored & thickly
   sliced
pesto, bought or homemade (see page 111)
aioli (see page 114)
parmesan, in the piece

Cook buns and tomato on the BBQ. Then put bun bottoms on a bench and smear generously with pesto. Top with tomato and mound vegies on top of that. Add a good dollop of aioli, some parmesan shavings and the lids.

Mixed vegies

... on a platter with salsa verde vinaigrette

1 cup basil leaves 1 cup Italian (flat leaf) parsley leaves 2 garlic cloves, crushed 1 tbsp capers, drained 3 anchovies	Whiz up in a blender or processor.
¼ cup olive oil ¾ tbsp Dijon mustard a good splash of balsamic vinegar sea salt & freshly ground pepper	Whisk in to above and set aside.

a variety of vegetables, such as finely sliced
   pumpkin, eggplant, zucchini, capsicum,
   mushrooms, fennel, asparagus and so on
olive oil spray
freshly ground salt & pepper
	Cut into neat shapes, oil well, season and barbecue until slightly charred and tender.

	Place on a platter and sprinkle with vinaigrette.

To add a smoky flavour to your food

on a gas-fired number, make a smoker pouch by placing soaked woodchips on a square of foil.

Wrap up tightly, poke a few holes in the top, then place under the grate over the burners.

Asparagus

... wrapped in prosciutto with horseradish sour cream

½ cup sour cream
1 tbsp creamed horseradish
1 heaped tspn snipped chives

Mix together and add boiling water, 1 teaspoon at a time, to achieve a thinnish consistency.

16 fat spears of asparagus, trimmed
  & peeled lightly

Bring a large pot of water to the boil, add asparagus and when it comes back to the boil immediately remove and plunge into a bowl of ice cold water. Leave to cool, then drain.

16 thin slices prosciutto
8 wooden skewers, soaked in cold water
  for 30 minutes

Wrap each spear of asparagus with a slice of prosciutto, then place 4 alongside each other on the bench. Push 2 skewers through crossways and repeat process. Barbecue on an oiled grill turning a few times until well coloured, then place on a plate (removing skewers if you like) and sprinkle with sour cream.

... with pesto oil & parmesan shavings

20 fat spears of asparagus, trimmed, peeled
  & blanched as above
8 wooden skewers, soaked in cold water for
  30 minutes
olive oil spray
freshly ground salt & pepper

Put 5 spears on 2 skewers as above. Spray well, season and barbecue, turning until well browned. Place on plates or a platter.

½ cup olive oil
1 heaped tbsp pesto, bought or homemade
  (see page 111)
parmesan shavings

Whisk oil and pesto together. Sprinkle over asparagus (serve any leftover on the side) and scatter with parmesan.

Beetroot

... in a salad with spiced yoghurt

Serve hot, warm or at room temperature.

8 medium-large beetroot, well scrubbed	Preheat kettle BBQ with direct heat (see page 50). Then wrap beetroot individually in foil and cook, covered, until tender when pierced with a knife. Allow to cool a little and then peel. (Using rubber gloves is not a bad idea as the juices do tend to stain your hands.)
a good squeeze of lemon juice **olive oil** **freshly ground salt & pepper**	While still hot, cut in wedges and toss with lemon juice, a good slurp of oil and seasonings.
½ cup plain yoghurt **½ tspn ground cumin** **½ tspn ground coriander** **1 heaped tbsp chopped fresh coriander** **a good squeeze of lemon juice**	Mix and, when ready to serve, mound on top of beetroot.

... baby beets with an orange glaze

Cut the tops off the beetroot only to about 1 cm of the bulb. If you cut any closer the beetroot will bleed.

16 baby beetroot, peeled **4 wooden skewers, soaked in cold water for 30 minutes** **olive oil spray** **freshly ground salt & pepper**	Put 4 beetroot on each skewer. Spray with oil, season and barbecue, turning regularly until tender when pierced with a knife.
½ small onion, chopped **1 cup fresh orange juice** **1 bay leaf** **5 whole black peppercorns**	While beetroot is cooking, combine in a small pot and cook down until a glaze is formed.
zest of 1 orange **chopped parsley**	Pour glaze over beetroot and sprinkle with zest and parsley.

Corn

... spicy barbecued sweet corn salsa

I often add extra oil to this and turn it into a salad with a robust lettuce
such as frissee or curly endive.

4 corn cobs, husk & silk removed **olive oil spray** **freshly ground salt & pepper**	Oil and season corn generously and barbecue until blistered in spots. Cool and then cut off kernels.
2 chillies, seeded & finely sliced **½ each red & green capsicum, seeded,** **cored & finely diced** **2 tbsp chopped fresh coriander** **juice of 1–2 limes**	Put in a bowl along with corn.
olive oil **freshly ground salt & pepper**	Add to taste.

... in the husk with lime & coriander butter

6 ears of corn in the husk	Pull back husk (but don't detach) and remove silk.
100 gm soft unsalted butter **juice of 1–2 limes** **2 tbsp chopped fresh coriander** **freshly ground salt & pepper**	Mix together, smear over corn and pull husk back over top. Tie with kitchen string and set aside until needed.
olive oil spray	Barbecue on the edge of the BBQ, rolling and spraying with oil frequently.
	Remove husk and serve with some extra butter.

If the husk is browning too much

put doubled-over foil underneath.

Cabbage

. . . in foil with bacon & onion

olive oil
3–4 rindless bacon rashers, sliced
2 large onions, chopped

Heat oil in a large pan and sauté until soft.

1 savoy cabbage, quartered & core cut out
olive oil spray
freshly ground salt & pepper
soft butter

Place cabbage quarters on four large oiled squares of heavy duty foil. Top with onion mix, seasonings and dabs of butter. Enclose tightly and barbecue, covered, until tender.

. . . spicy slaw with Thai flavours

The name coleslaw, to which this recipe is a distant relative, is German in origin. It was originally known as kohl slaw, which literally means cabbage sliced, but somewhere along the line kole was anglicised to cole.

½ wonga bok (Chinese white cabbage),
   finely shredded
1 medium carrot, coarsely grated
¾ cup torn mint leaves
3 tbsp cup pan-roasted peanuts (see page 4)
1 cup cubed fresh pineapple

Toss in a bowl.

2 tbsp Asian fish sauce
juice of 1–2 limes
1 tbsp rice vinegar
1 heaped tspn shaved palm sugar
3 chillies, seeded & sliced
1 garlic clove, crushed
3 tbsp vegetable oil

Whisk and add to taste.

Eggplant

... Keith Floyd's squidgy eggplant

I still consider the irrepressible, irreverent Keith Floyd to be the greatest TV chef. And this exceedingly simple recipe (from his book *Floyd on Fire*) is typical of his always approachable cooking style.

2 whole eggplants 1–2 garlic cloves, cut in slivers olive oil spray	Cut slits all over eggplants and slip garlic slivers in. Spray all over and barbecue, turning frequently until soft and squidgy.
extra virgin olive oil freshly ground salt & pepper lemon wedges	Cut in half lengthways and, with a spoon, mash in some oil and seasonings. Serve with lemon wedges.

... in a Turkish salad with coriander & lemon yoghurt

Can be served warm or at room temperature but never straight from the fridge.

2 cups olive oil 3 large eggplants, cubed	Heat oil in a wok or deep pan until smoking and, in 3 or 4 lots, fry eggplant until golden, draining well on kitchen towels.
1 large onion, chopped 2 garlic cloves, crushed	Drain off most of the oil and sauté until golden.
3 cans chopped tomatoes, drained a little ½ cup vegetable stock (bought is fine) a good pinch each cayenne & ground cloves 1 tspn each cinnamon, allspice & ground cumin freshly ground salt & pepper	Add and simmer gently for 15 minutes. Then add eggplant and simmer for another 5 minutes.
2 tbsp chopped fresh mint 2 tbsp chopped fresh coriander	Turn off heat and mix in.
½ cup plain yoghurt a good squeeze of lemon juice 1–2 tbsp chopped fresh coriander	When ready to serve, combine and sprinkle over the top.

Green beans

... with crumbled feta cheese

3–4 dozen baby green beans, topped
  & tailed
olive oil spray

Barbecue on a well-oiled BBQ until tender and lightly charred, spraying with oil as needed.

½ cup crumbled feta cheese
olive oil
balsamic vinegar
freshly ground salt & pepper

Put beans on a platter, season and sprinkle with cheese. Drizzle oil and vinegar over the top. Serve hot, warm or at room temperature.

... with almonds, brown butter & parmesan

3–4 dozen baby green beans, topped
  & tailed
olive oil spray

Barbecue on a well-oiled BBQ until tender and lightly charred, spraying with oil as needed. Put on plates or a platter.

a few good dollops of butter
1–2 tbsp blanched slivered almonds

While beans are cooking, put in a small pan on the hottest part of the BBQ and cook until brown. Pour over beans.

parmesan, in the piece

Grate over the top.

Barbecued beans are a great accompaniment

to any barbecued food. But they can also be served as part of a vegetarian selection

where their smoky flavours will delight.

Leeks

. . . with anchovies, extra virgin olive oil & balsamic

This recipe also works well with asparagus and witloof.

12–18 small leeks, well washed table salt	Blanch until crisp tender in a large pot of lightly salted water. Drain and pat dry.
olive oil freshly ground salt & pepper	Brush with oil, season and barbecue until lightly charred.
6 anchovies, chopped extra virgin olive oil balsamic vinegar chopped parsley	Put on a platter, scatter with anchovies and sprinkle generously with oil, balsamic and parsley.

. . . with bok choy & Asian flavourings

6–12 small leeks, well washed & halved crossways	Blanch until crisp-tender in a large pot of lightly salted water. Drain and pat dry.
vegetable oil 6 baby bok choy, cleaned, well washed & halved lengthways	Brush leeks and bok choy generously with oil and barbecue until lightly browned. Put on a platter.
1–2 garlic cloves, finely chopped 1–2 chillies, finely chopped soy sauce 2 tbsp vegetable oil 2 tspn sesame oil	Sprinkle vegies with garlic, chilli and a generous slurp of soy. Then, in a small pan, heat the oils until smoking and pour over the top.

Mushrooms

... field with garlic & herb butter

12–16 large field mushrooms olive oil spray freshly ground salt & pepper	Peel mushrooms and remove stalks. Spray all over with oil and season well. Throw on BBQ, white side up, and cook for 2–3 minutes.
100 gm soft unsalted butter 2 garlic cloves, crushed 1 heaped tbsp chopped parsley a squeeze of lemon juice	Mix together.
chopped parsley	Turn mushrooms over and place a dollop of butter in centre of each. Cook until they collapse a little. Then serve with a few more dollops of butter on top and a sprinkling of chopped parsley.

... in a sandwich with pesto & lemon mayo

³/₄ cup mayonnaise 3 tbsp sour cream juice of 1–2 lemons	Mix together, adding lemon juice to taste.
8 large field mushrooms olive oil spray 1 lemon freshly ground salt & pepper	Peel mushrooms and remove stalks. Spray all over with oil, season and barbecue, squeezing lemon over as you do so.
8 thick slices country-style bread pesto, bought or home made (see page 111) 1 handful baby rocket parmesan shavings	When mushrooms are ready, grill bread. Smear 4 slices with pesto, top with mushies, rocket, parmesan, lemon mayo and then the other bread slices.

Potatoes

... wrapped in foil with spring onions

16 baby spuds, scrubbed	Blanch in lightly salted boiling water until just tender. Drain well.
oil **2–3 spring (green) onions, chopped** **freshly ground salt & pepper** **butter**	Oil 4 squares of foil. Top with spuds, onions, seasoning and a knob of butter. Fold up, crimp edges and cook on BBQ.

... in my favourite potato salad

16 baby potatoes, scrubbed	Blanch in lightly salted boiling water until tender. Drain well and return to pot for a few minutes to dry out. Then cool and halve.
½ cup mayonnaise **3 tbsp sour cream** **1 tbsp Dijon mustard** **a squeeze of lemon juice**	Combine and, if needed, add boiling water a spoon at a time until consistency of a dressing.
olive oil **4 rindless bacon rashers, chopped** **4 spring (green) onions, cleaned & chopped**	Sauté bacon in a little oil until crispy and put in a bowl with potatoes and all the bacon cooking juices. Add spring onions and dressing to taste.

And a few more vegies

- To make potato shells, bake potatoes in microwave until tender. Halve lengthways and scoop out flesh leaving shell (reserve pulp for another use). Spray with oil, season and grill shells until crisp.

- Blanch whole onions in boiling water for 10 minutes then drain and cut in four. Spray with oil, season and cook on the slowest part of the grill until tender and charred.

- Peel baby carrots crossways and put them on two skewers. Then spray and barbecue brushing with a little butter and a sprinkling of nutmeg towards the end.

- Cut thin slices of pumpkin, spray and barbecue, brushing with golden syrup when almost ready.

- Slice a large eggplant into rounds. Oil, season and barbecue until tender and charred, then sprinkle with tzatziki (see page 112).

- Skewer cherry tomatoes and barbecue, brushing with garlic-flavoured olive oil as you do so.

- Try wrapping blanched sweetcorn in a double layer of foil with a dollop of butter and seasonings and then cooking buried in the coals themselves, turning once or twice.

- Wrap whole heads of unpeeled garlic individually in foil and cook for 45 minutes to 1 hour over a moderate heat. Squeeze flesh onto bread and add a splash of good olive oil.

- Barbecue thick slices of oiled, seasoned tomato briefly, then add a dollop of pesto.

- And last, but not least, bitter, hardy leaves such as radicchio also work well on the BBQ. Spray with oil, season and cook, turning regularly until tender and slightly charred all over (if large cut in half lengthways).

Today's barbecue

is an integral part of our
kitchen equipment and can
be used for everything from
family meals to special
dinner parties.

Potatoes

... in holy oil

½ cup olive oil
¼ cup fresh herb leaves (such as rosemary
    or thyme)
2 garlic cloves, crushed
1 chilli, seeded & finely sliced

To make holy oil, heat very, very gently in a pot until small bubbles appear. Remove from heat, set aside for 1 hour and then strain through muslin.

16 baby potatoes, scrubbed
freshly ground salt

Cook in lightly salted boiling water until just tender. Drain well and, when cool, halve. Brush with oil and barbecue, cut side down first, until crispy. Then toss with more oil and freshly ground salt.

While on the subject of potatoes

when using my kettle BBQ, I often wrap them individually in foil and throw them on the

coals (I also do this with sweet potatoes). Then all you need is a dollop of butter – delicious.

Tomatoes

... on charred bread with thyme, garlic oil & parmesan

½ cup olive oil
1 heaped tbsp thyme leaves
2 garlic cloves, crushed
freshly ground salt & pepper
4–6 ripe, red tomatoes, cored & halved

Mix oil, thyme, garlic and seasoning. Brush generously over tomatoes and barbecue on moderate part of the BBQ until tender and fragrant.

4–6 thick slices country-style bread
parmesan, in the piece

When tomatoes are ready, barbecue bread. Put on plates, top with tomato halves, a sprinkling of above oil and either shavings or freshly grated parmesan.

... barbecued tomato & red capsicum salsa

6 ripe tomatoes, cored, peeled and halved
    (see page 110)
olive oil spray
freshly ground salt & pepper

Oil and season generously and barbecue until lightly charred. Cool a little, chop and put in a bowl with any juices.

---

2 chillies, finely chopped
1 garlic clove, finely chopped
2 roasted red capsicums, diced (see page 110)
2 tspn chopped fresh thyme
olive oil
balsamic vinegar

Toss in bowl along with oil, vinegar and seasonings to taste.

Witloof

... with blue cheese

8 witloof, cleaned & halved lengthways
olive oil spray
freshly ground salt & pepper

Spray with oil, season and barbecue until tender and slightly charred.

½ cup olive oil
2 tbsp balsamic vinegar
1 tbsp seeded mustard
1 garlic clove, crushed
a pinch of sugar

Whisk together.

150 gm crumbled blue cheese

Put witloof on a platter, top with cheese and sprinkle generously with dressing.

... Witloof pickles

A recipe from one of the world's great chefs, Sydneysider Janni Kyritsis, these pickles are great with almost any barbecued food.

450 ml white vinegar
250 gm caster sugar
2 whole star anise
1 cinnamon stick, broken in 3
6 cloves

Put in a pot, bring to the boil and simmer gently for 30 minutes.

6 large witloof, trimmed & cut
  lengthways into 4

Put in a bowl and pour hot mix over the top. Cool, then refrigerate for at least 24 hours.

Also known as chicory and Belgian endive

the slightly bitter flavour of witloof works wonderfully on the barbie.

Wrapping it up

In the style of our better Chinese restaurants, I reckon there is nothing better than a large and exotic platter of fresh, cold fruit to finish off the feast. But do take note of the word 'exotic' and search out a few of the rarer varieties of fruit just to make that platter a little special (and resist the temptation to prepare the fruit hours in advance – it will be far better if prepared just before you serve it).

And whilst on the subject of fresh fruit platters, I recently had lunch at a friend's place and after the meal he served a large bowl of the most beautifully ripe fresh peaches – brilliant idea (and almost any perfect fruit could be used).

But if you are still, at this stage of the day, keen on showing off your barbecue prowess, keep in mind that almost any fruit benefits from a flash over the coals which invariably accentuates their sweetness and flavour. You can also, if you like, brush fruit lightly with honey towards the end of the cooking process just to help with the caramelisation. And what about a dunking sauce such as this butterscotch one which is made by combining 125 grams unsalted butter with 1 cup brown sugar (can be done in a pot on the BBQ) and once sugar is dissolved add 1 cup cream and simmer briefly (this works particularly well with bananas and pineapple). Or what about wrapping any fruits in foil along with orange juice, brown sugar and dark rum. Or cutting fruit into cubes and threading on skewers along with the odd marshmallow or two.

And, last but certainly not least, a great idea from my mate, Melbourne foodie Bob Hart: core some apples, stuff them with chopped up Mars Bars before wrapping them in foil along with a generous splash of Muscat. Throw them on a BBQ and cook them, turning once or twice, for 20–30 minutes. (Oh and I almost forgot, try making dessert pizzas by following the recipe description on page 84, but instead of a savoury topping, throw on some finely sliced ripe fruit and a sprinkling of sugar and, maybe, fruit liqueur.)

The basics

The basics are always what makes the difference between a good barbie and a great one. And, as you can see, few of these so-called 'gourmet tricks' are difficult to whip up. So, whilst I would be the first to admit that bought sauces, mustards and relishes are essentials, to me, so too are homemade butters, pastes and the like. And if you just happen to also whip up a batch of me mum's homemade tomato sauce, then special really is the catch cry for your next barbie.

How to

... roast a capsicum

For roasted capsicums, roast or grill halved capsicums until brown-black, cover with a roasting tray, kitchen wrap or a tea towel until cool, then core, seed and peel.

... peel a tomato

To peel and seed tomatoes, remove cores, put in boiling water and count to ten. Then plunge into iced water and cool. Peel and cut lengthways into quarters. Put on a board and cut out pulp (reserve pulp for another use). Dice flesh.

... de-beard mussels

To de-beard a mussel, grasp the string-like substance that grows out of the side of the shell and pull it towards the hinge end until it comes away.

Pastes

... pesto

15 basil leaves
1 garlic clove
2 tbsp grated parmesan
freshly ground salt & pepper
olive oil

Combine in a food processor, adding enough oil to make a thickish paste.

... harissa

4 tbsp coriander seeds
2 tbsp cumin seeds

Roast in a dry hot pan for a few minutes over a moderate heat.

6 tbsp olive oil
8 chillies, chopped
4 garlic cloves, chopped
freshly ground salt

Add and whiz up in a processor. (It will keep for a month in the fridge.)

Of course you can buy pastes

such as pesto and harissa but there is nothing quite like the homemade versions –

and, as you can see, they are pretty damned easy to make.

Sauces

... raita

1 cup plain yoghurt
1 large tomato, peeled, seeded & diced
  (optional, see page 110)
2 tbsp grated continental (telegraph)
  cucumber
1 heaped tbsp chopped mint
a squeeze of fresh lemon juice

Combine

... tzatziki

½ cup plain yoghurt
2 garlic cloves, crushed
2 tbsp chopped mint
a squeeze of lemon juice

Combine.

... harissa yoghurt

1/2 cup plain yoghurt
harissa (see page 111) to taste
2 tbsp chopped coriander
a squeeze of lemon juice

Combine.

Sauces

... me mum's homemade tomato sauce

Make this at least a few days in advance – it gets better with age. It's an absolute essential for any half decent barbecue.

2 kg ripe tomatoes, cored & roughly chopped
500 gm cooking apples, peeled, cored & roughly chopped
500 gm onions, peeled & roughly chopped
1¼ cups white vinegar
400 gm sugar
3 tspn allspice
2 tspn ground cloves
2 tbsp salt
good pinch cayenne
freshly ground black pepper

Put all ingredients in a heavy-bottomed pot, mix well and simmer for 1½ hours. Then blend, allow to cool, and put in sterilised jars or bottles (or, if you are using the sauce within a week or so, in a bucket in the fridge).

... Big Tex's BBQ sauce

3 cups tomato sauce
4 tbsp Worcestershire sauce
4 tbsp white vinegar
2 tbsp brown sugar
1 tbsp Dijon mustard
2–3 tbsp sambal oelek
4 garlic cloves, crushed

Pot in a heavy-bottomed pot, whisk well and simmer, gently, for 20 minutes.

What is a barbie without sauces?

And, as I may have mentioned, if they are homemade, even better.

Mayonnaise

... homemade mayonnaise

To make homemade mayonnaise, throw 2 eggs, 2 yolks, 1 tablespoon mustard and a pinch of salt into the food processor. Whiz up for one minute, then add 500 ml of any good oil, little by little, through the feeder tube. When all the oil is added, flavour to taste with fresh lemon juice and seasonings.

... anchovy mayo

½ cup mayonnaise
3 tbsp sour cream
4 anchovies, finely chopped
½ tspn Dijon mustard
1 tbsp chopped parsley

Mix ingredients (you may need to add a little hot water until it reaches a dressing consistency).

... aioli

½ cup mayonnaise
3 tbsp sour cream
1 tspn Dijon mustard
3 garlic cloves, crushed
a squeeze of lemon juice

Mix together.

... red capsicum aioli

1 red capsicum, roasted & peeled
  (see page 110)
½ cup mayonnaise
2 tbsp sour cream
1 tspn Dijon mustard
1–2 garlic cloves, crushed

Whiz up in a processor.

Butters

... Café de Paris butter

1 tspn chopped parsley
2 pinches paprika
2 pinches dried tarragon
1 tspn Dijon mustard
3 tbsp tomato puree
2 garlic cloves, crushed
4 anchovies
2 tspn capers, rinsed
6 pitted black olives

Whiz up in a processor.

---

500 gm soft unsalted butter
lemon juice
Tabasco
freshly ground salt & pepper

Add above to butter along with lemon, Tabasco and seasonings to taste. Mix well, then roll in foil and put in freezer until needed.

... garlic butter

250 gm soft unsalted butter
3 garlic cloves, crushed
1 heaped tbsp chopped parsley
a squeeze of fresh lemon juice

Combine, roll in foil and keep in freezer until needed.

I always make more of these butters than is needed, purely and simply because they add that touch of magic to any barbecued meat, poultry or seafood (and isn't it handy to have them sitting in the freezer?)

Accompaniments

... beetroot chutney

½ kg beetroot	Cook until tender. Then, when cool enough to handle, peel.
250 g onions	Coarsely chop onions and beetroot.
1 cup vinegar 1 cup sugar ½ tbsp rock salt ½ tbsp mustard seeds ½ tspn coriander seeds ½ tspn allspice berries, crushed freshly ground pepper	Put into pot along with onion and beetroot and gently simmer for 30-40 minutes until thick. Cool.

... tomato chutney

3 kg tomatoes, cored & roughly chopped 1 kg onions, roughly chopped 3 heaped tbsp salt	Put vegies in a large colander over a bowl and toss salt through. Refrigerate for 24 hours.
1 kg white sugar white vinegar	Put drained tomato mix in a large pot. Add sugar and almost cover with vinegar. Bring to the boil.
1 tbsp curry powder ¼ tspn cayenne 1 tbsp Dijon mustard 2 heaped tbsp sambal oelek	Add and simmer until fragrant and thick (adding a little water if necessary). Wonderful served with any plain grill.

Every barbecue needs a good chutney

and here are two of the best.

Index